The Automatic Hand

The Automatic Hand

Sad Glad Allah

AVON BOOKS
1 DOVEDALE STUDIOS
465 BATTERSEA PARK ROAD
LONDON SW11 4LR

Printed and bound in the U.K.

Avon Books

London

First Published 1997

ISBN 1 86033 222 6

Dedicated

To humanity, from someone who cares what happens to it.
And my thanks to God and his servants for making this possible.
Believe me, Man is the one at fault, not God.
And I bless my Wife and Son for the human qualities I've developed in my relationship with them on the path of truth and godism. And I thank all those people I met in my life as a traveller on the path of truth.
And peace and love to all believers of the world.

Contents

Introduction

The sixties was a very important time in our history as human beings, living on planet earth. Fortunately for mankind it was during that period when the almighty Creator re-established his link or (communion) with his creation again, after the Darwinian estrangement (or break with our Allah, the merciful) in the nineteenth century.

The sixties was the time of spiritual or (transcendental) awakening, and in the north west of London a few of us had received enlightenment and had transcended our animalistic psyche (which regulates the baser instinct in man) and were now on our human psyche, where I was catapulted to, (that regulates belief, hope, and trust) which leads to uprightness, in the pursuit of truth. So the sixties opened the way for the true search for the knowledge of our Creator on the path of truth.

Those of us who had reached the age of thirty years, (which is the age that every human being would have had their first calling under the divine ordinance of our Lord to the path of truth) would have decided, as we did, the road they chose to follow. We worked on ourselves and became more obedient to the laws of Allah and got to know him, and transcended to higher plains of perception and understanding. Whilst the others were led away by the famous musicians of the time, who were a little younger than ourselves, and who themselves were trying to put life in perspective, were open to the free love suggestion, and had fallen prey to the Gurus of the east, who probably meant well, but faced with the same opportunities of becoming as rich and famous as pop stars, continued the propagation of the gospel of free love, against what the enlightenment of the time was demanding, which was abstinence. Nevertheless the Gurus and the musicians with their allies the newspapers, radio, television and recording companies, had a great harvest at humanity's expense. That was also the time when parliament defied our beloved Allah, and legalised homosexuality amongst consenting adults and the Church of England condoned and sanctified this act, knowing full well, that it was sacrilege to do so. At that time also, the world superpowers were threatening mankind with annihilation, and any political leader who hadn't the constitution to press that doomsday button was not looked upon favourably by their colleagues, so with the threat of destruction hanging over the heads of the sixties generation, they were seduced by the devil's advocates down the wrong path of life, which was really a horrid time for the thinker for we couldn't stop the crest of the wave that led to the present world situation. We also saw the breaking up of family units and the young people began to see their parents for the first time and did not like what they saw, for their elders were the baddies of the time, as the teenagers, we are told, are the baddies of today. Although they were less frightening than their fathers and mothers were in the sixties and seventies, for they wanted to obliterate mankind for the sake of an idea.

Autobiography

My search for the truth started in the year 1964 when I first asked myself what was life all about. The answer then seemed remote, for my life up to that time was one of pleasure, which I sought at every waking moment. After I'd left my job in 1962, I suppose one could say that I was a man around town, because I indulged in all the vices regardless of the time of day, and God was far away from my mind. Although I had a conventional religious upbringing which I rejected at the age of twelve one Sunday morning after being forced out of bed by my sister (who happened to be a very religious person) to attend high mass. Faced with the question of what life was all about and not having the answer, I decided to find out. For no one seemed to have the answer, nor even the hierarchy of the various religious denominations, as I soon found out after making it my duty to listen to the epilogues and symposiums by the intellectuals on television. Of course there were valid points made by them, but not adequately profound to this vital question, which by this time was driving me near to suicide; for my life seemed empty, nothing seeming to hold my interest.

One day I happened to go into the West End for no particular reason, and ran into a friend of mine who was on his way to Foyles bookshop, and he asked me to accompany him. I had never bought a book in my life before, although I'd read a few to no avail. Anyhow, I decided to purchase one, and bought one on English Grammar, although I had no idea how this book was going to help me find the answer to my question, which no one had the answer to.

Nevertheless, I applied myself slowly and diligently in spite of my environment, until my mind became alive. But, now I was confronted with more questions that every so-called intelligent person had already answered. I then became interested in politics during the general election of 1964, and read every political article written in the newspapers of the three major parties, assessing everything that was said. I followed the campaigns on television to the very end, but remained unattached to any of the parties. By this time I had already comprehended the definitions of the names of the contending parties and the desire of belonging to one of them took a hold of me. So I put myself under scrutiny and found my disposition to be liberal and free-thinking, until one night while looking at television I suddenly heard these words in my head: "I am the Lord thy God." I jumped out of the chair that I was sitting in, and felt an inner eye in my head looking down at me; my heart began to race but I soon settled down to the realisation that I had found God, and from then on he has been my teacher, although from time to time I took this intelligence for granted until he first relinquished it.

My speech would suddenly stop in company, my mind would become foggy, the light would dim, and the only thought in my mind would be to get home as fast as I could. The first time that this happened to me I thought that I was being repudiated by him. I remember now how I cried and begged him to return to me, for without him I was lost and had no one to help me, for my friends at the time had it about that I was mad, which in a sense I was responsible for. For one day I was returning home from a friend I'd visited at Notting Hill Gate and had overstayed the time permitted to me by God speaking on a subject that had no relevance to my life at the time. You may wonder what the subject was so I will tell you: what do ordinary men speak about except women? My speech was cut off and that brought the end to my visit, so you can imagine me in my desperation to get home to my meditation and frozen to complaining point on one of those sunless days with the rain descending and the cold biting one's body, running in to another friend of mine. I became apprehensive on seeing him from a distance and would have turned down some other street if it was possible, but I had no choice. He came over from the opposite side of the street and greeted me with "What's happening, man?" So I told him that I was being punished by God.

All this had passed and I still hadn't realised that I had become a mystic. My first command from God was to stop smoking which I did without hesitation, with a strict warning to adhere to my meditation and studies. After this warning my isolation began. I read books that I was directed to and for one year I remained in solitude. I neither bathed myself or ate anything substantial, sleep was denied me, but rest I had plenty of. I meditated all day long, sometimes in a trance, until I was all mind and no body. By this time my relationship with the girl that I lived with had begun to deteriorate. She began to despise me for denying her her rights. She also was convinced that I was mad.

All this time it seemed to me that I was sitting in a glass globe and seeing the world for the first time. Every thing became crystal clear, although I could not put it in words. I was examining democracy and its product, communism and its product, and decided against both systems, and the thought of becoming a politician was erased from my mind. Machiavellianism was not for me, for I was after the truth, and phase one of my solitude came to an end. I realised now that I had found myself when I found God and was ready to face the world once more, so I ventured out in the summer of 1965 for the first time to find my ankles just about able to support my weight, but happy to be alive and well. My walk took me to Hampstead Heath, where I sat on a hill overlooking the little village that seemed deserted to me. Only the sky, the clouds and the trees seemed to command my attention, and I was at peace with the world. I sat there for hours, and when I decided to leave my thought became poetic and I said: "I've seen the trees dancing today as the wind engulfed them on its way. Each tree doing a dance of its own trying not desperately, but gracefully to out-dance each other, and oh, how did these trees dance with such rhythm that I had never seen with their branches swaying and their leaves performing a thousand variations of the dance, and as the wind subsided these trees took their former stance, breathless awaiting to start again their sacred dance." I maintained this thought on my journey home.

A few weeks later a very dear friend of mine came to see me. He being a student at Christ Church College was amazed to find me so well informed, although I found his concept of life somewhat distorted. He seemed quite pleased with himself, for after all he had acquired his O levels and now he was in an environment where he was being conditioned to take his place in society, and he tried to encourage me to do the same, for he thought I was wasting time, if I was going to study at home and at the end of my studies had no certificates to hold up to the world.

I was liberally minded now in my outlook but my future seemed remote, although I had a good idea where in society I would fit in, so I decided to become a composer. I had already composed a few songs some years ago, so I said to myself I'll brush them up a bit and try my luck. By this time I'd forgotten all about God but was still living a clean life, but in complete ignorance of the spiritual elevation that I had achieved. Then suddenly God made his demand. I had to surrender myself to Him. I hesitated for about two to three minutes, then I surrendered. I expected immediate results, but nothing spectacular happened except for a calm satisfaction and a peaceful night's sleep.

The next morning I awoke and went about my business as usual, with the desire of becoming a composer still foremost in my mind. Eventually I bought a tape recorder and taped my songs. I tried then to get a few persons interested in my work but without any results. Then my domestic troubles began. My woman became pregnant and my life became a misery. The equanimity I had achieved began to diminish, our verbal battles became virulent and relentless, and then one day I accepted the fact that I was to become a father and so our battles ceased. Finance we had none, but somehow I knew we were going to pull through. I found myself a job and accepted my responsibility. Soon after this she was hospitalised for three months because of complications. The time was drawing near for her to give birth but the baby still hadn't turned.

We had a daughter in June of '66, and very proud of her we were. We both adored her, our relationship began to improve, but then I became retrospective, living constantly in the past, a past I had forgotten. I was like a victim of amnesia whose memory had begun to confront him. I could not communicate with anyone, not even the woman I lived with. I remained reticent for how long I don't know, for time meant nothing to me. This was too much to ask an inexperienced girl to undergo. She tried to penetrate my meditation with suggestions both kind and absurd. At this stage the past had possessed my mind, I was reliving my early life and she was not part of it.

"Mac" or "Darling" she would call out to me from time to time, but I could not reply, for we lived in two different dimensions, she in the present where I no longer belonged except physically. God had taken hold of me again, I was going through the phase of analytical meditation.

After this phase, almost two years passed by with no direct communication from God. We had gone our separate ways, or so I thought, and I continued to live my life without conscious communication as best as I could, still holding on to my faith. I noticed too that my intelligence had ceased to be on the level to which I had become accustomed, although my reasoning remained the same. This was my first serious spiritual fall. I went through the period of my designation with a mental blockage, telling myself I must straighten my life. I had no idea what the result was going to be, for I hadn't read mysticism. I finally found a place that suited my temperament and commenced to find the equanimity that was necessary. Miracles began happening, a veil lifted from my eyes and I saw the star that I was born under, and the spiritual beam that connects the cosmic chamber of the brain. I immediately started sending out telepathic messages. By the time I got home, I had received the ring of protection which I projected around me for my safety, for I was now in the spiritual reality. My first task was to write about the Devil, which you will come to in the third chapter of this book.

I had already undergone all the necessary tests of courage. I had faced death, I'd confronted the Devil, so I began to write. I finished writing about him in one night. My work was an inspired dictation from God, and the whole spiritual mechanism of the universe opened up before my eyes and I was in the spiritual straight in direct communication with God. I was initiated and now a true mystic, which is the normal way of life, for a man is supposed to be in communion with God and not the Devil.

I began to live the life of a mystic in complete harmony with the universe, taking my direction from God and keeping a constant watch in the sky for signs. On the third of September 1968, on a clear moonlit night I stood at my window looking at the moon and it vanished before my eyes. Two days later the sun bowed in reverence to my purity, then one night, two weeks after these miracles, my astral travels began.

When God came into being from the phenomena that he evolved from he meditated and achieved his accomplishment. He had no teacher, He was not even aware of his potentiality. Gradually he developed into the supreme being and created the universe, and this was the beginning.

Death and its Significance

Most people are afraid to think of death, but death is the beginning of new life; for one's spiritual self never dies, as I found out during the period of profound meditation and astral projection. It was only then that I became aware of my true self, which is far more godlike in its make-up than my physical self, and realised that we are lost souls on our way to hell. When anyone dies unpurified, the spirit goes to the plane of lost souls for a period of time, awaiting re-entry into a body here in hell, and goes through the same process as before until the new body which it occupies becomes aware, and this awareness could take hundreds of years, especially because of the rejection of God due to the hypocrisy of the church's superficial doctrines, and man's inability to think for himself.

But the plane of lost souls is not the only place in the universe; for there are other planes for the more enlightened spirit, which few of us happen to ascend to. If the purification of a man's spiritual self is at the level of a king angel, he ascends to the plane of giants and will see with his own eyes the perfect body that awaits him there: and when he dies during this period of purification and spiritual awareness he is released from the death cycle here, that leads to hell, to the plane of his purity: a purity which is also necessary to maintain for astral travels to various planes of the spiritual reality which is unknown in the Western world.

Astral travels, as I found out, require the highest purity and a purity that requires the highest discipline, for it is only when this purity was acquired that my travelling became frequent, and what I thought at first was an illusion later revealed itself to me as the spiritual reality (which Lobsang Rumpa described in his books) and the enlightenment of life after death, which is a subject avoided in this backward place hell, was revealed to me and as a servant of God it becomes my duty to pass it on to you.

The road to hell is very much like a maze and it took me quite some time to release myself from it, as the pleasures that lead to hell are very enticing but short-lived. Even the landscapes and seascapes in hell have their deceptive beauty. If a man is placed in this maze and he's contented to remain there, then there's nothing anyone can do to help him, but if he's interested in discovering the way out of the maze he will start looking for a way out while shouting for the keeper, except in this case the Devil is the maze keeper, so for a man to achieve his emancipation he has to call the highest authority which in this case is God.

DEATH AND BIRTH

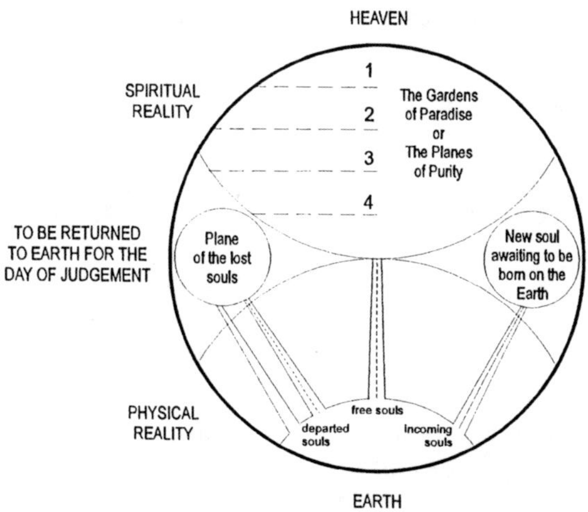

When the righteous
Soul has ended its time here
on this cruel earth,
And begins its journey
back to its lord, from
Where it once embarked,
Through the cosmos it
journeys on with Angels
At its side taking it to
the new abode on high.

THE MAZE OF HELL

THE ONLY WAY OUT, IS TO ASCEND!!

After one is released from the maze of hell, which is not very easy to accomplish, then and only then will the person see the true light and become perceptive of the shrewd expediency of the Devil in every trace of the democratic and communist systems, as these two systems and all the false doctrines that we adhere to, are the ingenuity of the Devil .

Man is either an instrument of God or the Devil, and I prefer to be an instrument of God than of the Devil, for he, or it, is a force of greater confusion which is so noticeable in every transaction in the societies of the world. Modern science has gone out on a very precarious limb in deceiving mankind with its technological achievement, but here again it is apparent that the ingenuity of the Devil is using man as an instrument to achieve his goal in defying God and his laws of nature.

The Forces of Nature

The forces of nature are many, but it is up to man to search for the right force to control his life; but first he must learn to recognise them. A wise man always chooses the force of divinity, for this is the force of miracles and eternal light, and his evolution begins the transitionary change from ordinary man to human and Godly being. So it is clear that man has a choice to change if he wishes, but he has no desire to do so and makes excuses, but inevitably the change has to come from the heads of state, for it is there that the forces of evil are most active, as is so very clear to see from the spiritual reality.

The Physical Reality

Now let us examine the physical reality in the form of the two systems men are forced to be submissive to. First we'll take communism because it's the youngest of the two systems, and examine the reason why it will never work, in spite of the fact that it is the more humane of the two systems and is in the poor man's favour. Would the offspring of the autocrat allow communism to work? After all, the system is only fifty* years old and the offspring of the autocrat and noble families can still remember what life was like in the past, and their parents surely would have passed down the autocratic doctrine which from time to time comes to the surface: resulting in a few of them, whenever the opportunity arises, coming over to the West and seeking political asylum and promulgating propaganda, which the western powers gratify themselves in, as this treacherous behaviour serves as a buoy to democracy, strengthening western propaganda against communism, which the unenlightened proletariat consume like a tonic and the capitalists lavishly bath themselves in. I ask you, has any poor Russian defected to the West? Surely not, and if he did, no doubt he would be an idiot to do so.

So you find the restrictive characteristics of communism are necessary until the conditioning process has evolved, but the metamorphosis will extend to several generations, never becoming an inertia because of the constant threat of the autocratic offspring, which communist China took the necessary precaution to avoid by assassinating their offspring whenever the occasion arose. But this atrocious behaviour is internal and had absolutely nothing to do with the West, for, as the Englishman says, a man's home is his castle.

* *Communism has now been in use for seventy years.*

Now let us direct our thoughts to the prerogative dominance of communism on the smaller communist countries and compare it with the democratic prerogative dominance over the smaller democratic countries and all the other facets inherent in the two systems when it comes to foreign affairs. A very good example of the two systems at work was in Vietnam in South East Asia. In 1968, and more recently with the American invasion of Grenada in complete disregard of the suffering of the inhabitants, we saw a magnificent exhibition of the two systems' atrocious, treacherous and murderous behaviour and of the ordinary human animal's incapability, in spite of his technological achievement, to live in peace. Yet these two systems hold our lives on the press of a button. With true religion absent in the world, may God help us.

Democracy at Work

Let us look at democracy in all its glory. Its definition means that form of government in which the sovereign power resides in the people, or government by the people, and basically freedom, which the ordinary man defines it as, but freedom to do what? His only freedom lies in the fact that he is free to associate with either of the three parties whose manifestos show no differentiation, so it doesn't really matter which of them is elected to govern the country. And although elected by the people, the government goes through a transition back to the sovereign adhesive to the old remedies as the panacea for all economic and social ills, and caters for the affluent and middle class families, repudiating its responsibility to the proletariat.

I am ashamed of man, except for the humanist who ascend to the spiritual plane of the hippogriffs when he dies, for he is half human and half animal.

So clearly the next system must be humanistic in structure with strong overtures to Godlinism and astral meditation foremost in its curriculum, for as long as man remains an animal the Devil will always be able to distort his judgement.

The Mind's Eye

The mind's eye, which is referred to as the third eye, is a section of the brain that is completely separated from that part of the brain that stores information that we collect during our education, but is dormant in most of mankind and is the section where communication with God begins and is also the receiver and transmitter of telepathic communication and is a direct link to the universal bodies.

The computer that the scientist proclaims to be a copy of man's mind is a replica of the lower intellect of the brain which puts out nothing more than it receives, and sometimes a lot less that it receives. Most people's minds are attuned to accepting false doctrines and rejecting true ones, but the reason for this is simply that their minds are trained from early life by the force of distortion, so that later in life their minds refuse to comprehend the truth, and that's the world's trouble today and the reason for the darkness we live in.

I sit in my room and see the world racing expeditiously to its final chapter like a Frankenstein about to strike its master and the master completely unaware of his end, and a special joy and depression overwhelms me, the joy because I know that the time is near for the righteous to take over the world, the depression because of the unworthy that will pass away without seeing the light.

The world is divided into four groups of people, the believers, the atheists, and those who don't know what to believe; but the inquirers are the ones who find God and, with the acknowledgement of him, become the righteous that are so often scoffed at by the ignorant who brands them fanatics. But I shall never forget the day of my wakening when I ventured out to see the bishop of the catholic church to inform him that I had found God and to my realisation discovered in the precinct of his domain the evil that dwells there, and thoughts of my youth when I was a regular attendant of the church and complied to all its rules flashed through my mind, and now confronted with its evil, panic rose in me for I felt the divine light that was shining in my mind started to dim and I had to get away from the precinct as fast as I possibly could. The thought of going to the devil's advocate with the news or my divinity sends shivers down my spine even today.

So when I say that there is a true God and a false God I know what I'm talking about.

Many men have had the divine calling that I've had but lost it in their ignorance by turning to some religious institution, which I myself would have done had I not seen the true light because of the purity of my thoughts which I maintained during my darkness, for I too once lived in the darkness that the world is in at present. But my travels to the starry planet, the sun, the moon, and the plane of the angels confirmed that God is present in man and that we are of him and he's of us, but because of our many activities we are unaware of his presence. I speak to God as a friend and father, I embrace him as a lover, we share jokes that only he and I could understand, we have our rows, we console each other, we cry together, in fact we love each other and there are always ecstatic moments. I know of no comedian, black, white or yellow that can make me laugh the way he does.

Sagacious though they may be,
The light of wisdom shines not their way,
For stumble in the dark they must
Like bats in the light of day.

Conflict of the Mind and what causes it

The first sign of conflict in the mind is due to doubt and lack of understanding of the process which is taking place in the person's mind, which results in a complete breakdown or the loss of faith in God. When this occurs the person is in the hands of Baal, or the Devil, and this means ruination of the soul. Democracy is responsible, but the person could be saved providing he seeks a true servant of God, which is not difficult, for God's servants are always directed to such a person and bound to oblige.

If two persons are living under the same roof and cannot agree, this creates conflict in the home, and finally ends in divorce, so it is impossible for both spirits to dwell in harmony in the same body. God created man and woman, as all believers know, but before he could give the secret of everlasting life and happiness to them, the Devil planted his seed of disobedience in woman and man, and this is how the Devil entered into man and changed things, but the secret is now revealed, which we will come to later on in this holy work.

How to Eradicate the Devil

To achieve this, man must first learn to recognise him or it, for the Devil is a highly intelligent beast but insane and the enemy of man and a very busy body, whose sole purpose is to detain us all in hell, which for the moment is earth.

The first thing a person must do is become just in everything that he does, because God is a just God and he adheres to a just man, but the devil despises a just man, and tempts him all the more. So one has to be on the look-out all of the time, for he uses very shrewd approaches. And the early attempts to eradicate him take a bit of doing.

We have already established the presence of the Devil in the body. So every friend, every relative, every acquaintance is used as an instrument; he will even stoop as low as using a child, and that proves how desperate he wants company in hell. Can you imagine all of God's children ascending to heaven and leaving him in hell alone? So this is why one has to be more than careful until recognition of him becomes a cinch.

Every good-natured person possesses more of God in him than the bad-natured person, who possesses more of the Devil, but even a good-natured person has a little of the Devil in him which sometimes comes to the surface. Such a person could easily eradicate the Devil, but it is tremendously hard for a bad-natured person to accomplish this, and God remains dormant and humiliated, biding his opportunity. Both parties remain unaware of these two forces, but God is by far the strongest. It is only when you seek him that he takes over and helps you to eradicate the Devil.

Now if you wish to please God, do to your neighbour as you would have your neighbour do unto you, but if your neighbour does unto you the things that you would not anticipate doing unto him, he is possessed by the Devil. You leave him alone until he changes his ways.

Recognition of the Devil

As a novice, on meeting a stranger, or even a friend or relative, first ask him, if he believes in God. If he says yes, ask him which of the Gods he believes in, for there are two. The true God, and the false

God. Now anyone who likes money more than his neighbour and will do anything to get it, believes in the Devil, which is the false God, but the true God loves kindness, honesty, and justice, and if you practice these neighbourly acts and he does not, run like hell, for if you delay he will contaminate you all over again. In conversation with a group of people the Devil is the one who does all the opposing with the false philosophy he read or acquired from some other Devil like himself. For the Devil's advocates are always present, but never stop to reason.

When the government meet at their summit meeting, there is where you have the most opposition, for here are all the Devils together, and without any representative of God in their midst they castigate each other, never reaching an agreement, no matter how important the issue at stake. Emphatically speaking, the king of Devils is a serpent, and if men are so stupid as to adhere to the teachings of a creature, it shows why the world will have no peace, for men will only become wise when they have the master God as their teacher.

The pupils of God are few, in the midst of the world population, so the few devils you meet in the path of life are no different from the Devils of other parts of the world, for they all serve the same Devil, as all God's servants serve the same God.

After you have mastered the ways of recognising him, it becomes both ludicrous and pathetic to see the tremendous effort he makes to avert your course. Frankly speaking, we are living in a world of fools, and this applies to the heads of states in this modern day and age, and the world of fools becomes your entertainers, so any man who wishes to remain in this state conforms to society. It does not matter if you allow a socialist, conservative, liberal, or Communist party to be in office, for they all exercise the Devil's philosophy, which is lies and corruption, but they the members are not responsible, for mankind was conditioned by the Devil into accepting him and remained completely unaware of it.

The Regulation of Weather

Human behaviour controls the weather and causes whatever disaster comes with it and turns around and blames God. The universe is comprised of invisible and spiritual mechanisms which are directed or connected to the souls of men, and attached to various clock gauges, or Atom Copus, which register the evil doing of men, and when the hands of these gauges make a complete turn the punishment destined for that particular sin comes, such and such a sin for floods, earthquakes, hurricanes, volcanoes, plagues, and the rest. But men see this the other way around, and think the weather controls their behaviour, when it's really their behaviour that controls these phenomena.

> *Sura XLII - 30*
> Whatever misfortune happens to you is because of the things your hands have wrought and for many (of them) He grants forgiveness.

Adam and Eve Misfortune and our Carnal Love

If two persons are in love with each other and both are of the same temperament which is to say of the same false God, their relationship reaches an equilibrium of great satisfaction during sexual intercourse, which pleases the Devil, but displeases God, for the simple reason that it does not reach the level of ecstasy he intended it to. There are differences of degrees of God and the Devil in men and women, and if one finds the corresponding degree of God or the Devil in his or her partner, their marriage works out fine, but if not, their relationship is always tense, resulting in either partner withdrawing from the other, and becoming an adulterer or an adulteress, and despising each other.

Spiritual Love

Spiritual love, which is the hardest of all love to acquire and the love that God intended for human beings, is the greatest love and blessed are the man and woman that acquire this kind of love for they dwell in paradise. For spiritual love is life everlasting, and the love that God intended for human beings, and Adam and Eve did not wait for it because of the Devil.

How to Acquire Spiritual Love

To acquire spiritual love the couple have to eradicate the Devil, and surrender themselves to God. To achieve this is not easy, but it is not impossible, as I said before there's two spirits that motivate man, the good and the evil, and if the couple co-operate in harmony to please each other, in every way and at all times, being just, honest, and considerate, the Devil will leave them both (never to return) and God shall take his rightful place, and they shall enjoy paradise, and become one in the eyes of God. This is called spiritual marriage, which no man could put asunder, and if he tries to, he will surely die, for what God has joined together is everlasting. This applies to courting couples as well, for when the couple reaches the spiritual plane God performs the marriage. For the marriage that is performed by man in these times is not valid in the eyes of God.

Complete Eradication

One has to be a nonconformist to the state, for the state is the main instrument of the Devil. The Sophist doctrine, which is the foundation of the democratic system, has nothing to do with God, and it was under such a system that Christ rebelled and tried to open the citizens' and peasants' eyes, and was prosecuted by the state, for he was a righteous man, as I am, a man of God who could not stand injustice. The state then pretended to have accepted his teaching and bamboozled the citizens and peasants back into the pagan system and distorted his teachings. The cross and its symbolical significance is ironical, its function is a reminder to any man who becomes aware of his duty to God, and it represents a direct threat as a deterrent to all men who seeks true justice for mankind. Christ didn't die because of his love for mankind, for what is there of mankind for any one to love? Christ sacrificed his life because of his love for his maker, and he doesn't want mankind to worship him. What he wants is for mankind to be like him, but how could they, when they are contented to remain sub-human?

The anthropologist, psychologist, scientist, and hierarchy have all made their contributions in misguiding mankind, but at their levels of perception they too are misled, and therefore cannot be held responsible. The anthropologist claimed that "man is an animal" in 1861 and mankind accepted this. The psychologist determined our conditioning, but we remain unaware of this, while doing exactly as he dictates. The scientist produced devastating weapons to destroy mankind and we praised him for it. The hierarchy induce fear in our minds about hell and damnation, when we are already on the road that leads to hell. So this also makes it necessary for me to reveal my discoveries at this level of perception.

Man's imitation of the animal kingdom, as I discovered, has changed his characteristics to such an extent that it's unbelievable. His characteristic is a combination of the behaviour of the various species of animals, and he has shifted from his psychic plane onto theirs, and he is now controlled by the forces of the animal galaxy. And so his behaviour is in pattern with the lower cosmic plane, which governs the animal kingdom, which early man copied in the process to find his way after turning away from God. Any man who thinks profoundly stands a good chance of slipping back to the psychic plane of the almighty God.

But with our lack of knowledge of the spiritual reality, we pronounce him as being mad, oblivious of the scientists who have made it possible for man to destroy himself.

The upper and middle classes are never much trouble to any state for they are to busy trying to be like each other. You have the upper class emulating the bureaucrat, the middle class emulating the upper class, and each only seeing the façade of each other, but they are all fools and instruments used by the Devil for his ultimate aim of defying God the holy and Most Highest King and Father of us all. But woe to them, when the time comes, which is much sooner than they think, for it is written in the sky for those who have the heavenly eyes to see.

The religion of peace was the catalyst which Christ innovated, as any man completely free of the Devil would have done, and which I am doing at this moment, exposing the fallacy of the democratic states and the misguidance of the monarchy which God and I detest, and the government of heaven is troubled about. Christianity is referred to as a religious cult, but in the days of Christ it was the political manifestation which caused the attempted assassination, and a great mistake by humanity.

Man's only hope now is for him to get back to his psychic plane or suffer the consequences of his lack of wisdom, which my brother Christ brought him and was castigated for. This is the last warning of our heavenly father.

The Government of God

The recommended system is Godism, and under this system all men are equal, professional-wise, as well as citizen-wise. If this is not adequately clear then I shall expound it. Let us compare a doctor's work with that of a dustman. If there were no dustmen there would be more diseased persons for the doctor to attend to, and he would be kept so busy he would not have time to scratch and eventually he himself would become a victim of the disease, so in the eyes of God they're both equal and deserve the same consideration, and the same applies to the employer and the employee. The employer needs the employee, as the employee needs the employer and they become dependent on each other and are therefore equal and deserve the same consideration in relation to salaries, with the residual profits going to the state for the benefit of all.

The various industries of the world would fix a maximum and equally a minimum wage structure according to their economic position, and the richer countries should subsidise the poorer countries with no strings attached, for with this system there would not be wars or any of the sinful actions which cause them, such as treachery, political deceit, political greed, political bullying, and diplomatic peeping toms, for all these snake-in-the-grass actions are a disgrace and shameful in the eyes of God, and the work of the Devil, and could play no part in Christ Government.

Education

Every citizen would be given a true spiritual education with God as the head teacher and the earthly archangels as servants to assist the pupils if required. The professional trade would be taught by angels who are qualified servants of God, and eventually all conventional apparatus would play no part in our lives, for with God as the head teacher mankind would no longer be animals and would become spiritual beings and their reward would be ecstatic and plentiful.

The Laws of the State

The ten commandments which the Lord thy God gave to Moses must be observed and adhered to at all times, and the plagues of this hell earth shall disappear altogether and the children of God shall become beautiful, for with the cleansing of their inner selves their external selves will be beautified tenfold. You shall all become vegetarians and eat live protein, fruits and the heavenly food of our father, and turn away from the Devil's highly seasoned food and the dead meat that you eat now, for your bodies are the burial ground for dead beasts, which must be put to an end.

The Devil's Plight to get back to Heaven

The Devil's effort to get back to heaven is ludicrous. At the moment he's trying all his technological skill to establish residence on the moon, and from there, on to heaven, but the heavenly barrier and spiritual bodies shall teach him a lesson. The reason for his unrelenting effort is because he knows that the time is drawing near for his damnation, so up he keeps sending these monstrous rockets reconnoitring space, but the archangels are watching his misconception. He keeps promulgating to the world that there are valuable minerals which could be of great use to man (in other words the imps or sub-humans of this hell earth) but even if he gets there and started transporting minerals it would mean disaster, for the excess weight of the minerals on this hell earth is sure to tilt the earth. But he's too foolish to even contemplate this. The truth is he's preparing to take off from earth when the time comes and run away leaving all his believers behind to perish, excepting of course his high-ranking subordinates and their families. And if this is not a good insight of the kind of serpent you all worship, and if you refuse to take heed of what I have said, then you shall surely perish along with the Devil, which the world seems not to be aware of.

The Devil's Religions

All the religious institutions of the world are false and are recognised by God as commercial and brain-washing industries. Their true function is keeping the people foolish and extracting the little money the poor people have and causing them more suffering and guiding them to hell, for their prayers are for money and money becomes their God.

The origin of confession in the Roman Catholic church was simply to keep in touch with what was going on among the people of the state, but your true church is internal and the pastor that dwells there is authentic, and he cares not to restrict your desires but to fulfil them, so let your religion be your intelligence and reasoning, but impartial reasoning on the path of the prophets in the religion of truth.

Meditation and the Future

Going to the past to straighten one's future by meditation as memory allows and reaching the spiritual planes, one has to go down the years of one's life examining, reasoning and asking for forgiveness for all the wrong things one has done, even as far back as childhood. As a child you are not responsible for the things you have done, but now in maturity you have a good picture of yourself and how wicked you were then, so you repent for those early years of your life, and come back to the present, so straightening your future and racing on to heavenly bliss.

To achieve this you have to be retrospective, using your memory as a vehicle to travel to the past as far back as memory would allow, stopping at all the stations of life, assessing one's behaviour with the uttermost sincerity and truth, asking for forgiveness of one's atrocious behaviour and forgiving others for their atrocities towards you. This process lightens the heart, and makes it possible for you to love your neighbour and even to forget about yourself during the course of travel, for one is cogitating on one's actions and not on one's self and ascending expeditiously on an upward journey towards God. It's inevitable to travel through the past for your journey of the future because your future is above you and not preceding you; what really lies ahead are your gains.

So cleansing one's inner self is imperative and far more important than mammon; these are the true words of God.

As a sub-human, man has a soul, but no conscience. And without a conscience he is lost, and destined to perish like a blighted tree, and diminish like a grain of sand in an ocean of darkness. And all because he has forgotten God his creator who gave him life and all the amenities to sustain it. Our father is sad because of the way we have been treating him, yet he has been taking care of us from the time 288,000 light years to this day, simply because man has not been able to develop his true potentialities, to take the responsibility on his shoulders, which can only be obtained by the opening of the Third Eye. When our father created us, he meant for us to be wholeheartedly like him, righteous and wise; he endowed in our souls nine intellectual planes (or levels) of perception. So far we have only been able to develop four, and this is very dissatisfying to our souls. Bertrand Russell, the greatest of all the western philosophers of the twentieth century, just about managed to ascend to two of the other levels of perception, and was three levels away from meeting God, with the point of decision just above him, and two levels above that of the ordinary man, but he missed the chance of becoming a mystic. He was not spiritually awakened to the point of acknowledgement, and was caught up in the materialistic philosophy (of Berkeley, Locke, Bacon, et al, advocates of the Devil) and so failed to achieve his future, which is sad. And with most of mankind five levels of perception away from God our Father, it is very clear, then, the darkness the world is in, and the sorrow we are causing our Father who loves and cares for us so much. Yet we despise his name, and turn to the Devil, who possesses the Knowledge of a snake.

If the world would stop all its activities for two days of silence, our Father would make his presence felt, so that we could acknowledge him. Is it too much to ask of his children? I for one do not think so. He has left it to the nations of the world to fix a date for two days of silence, and promised to take care of the sick in hospital, believers as well as non-believers, six months after the publication of this book. I beseech you all to accede to our Father's request.

Stagnation of Religion

The religious institutions, that remained at the novice stage of lamentation, have become stagnated through fear. This lamentable stage is the purifying process of the soul for further scientific discoveries of the four higher worlds, which allows one to penetrate the boundary of fear, and go on to the science of spiritual evolution and the plane of the higher worlds.

It's important that fear should be eradicated from the soul, which can only be attained by purification, through the early stages of mysticism, ascending the spiritual straight, and the science of spiritual evolution which is the source of wisdom, acquired by divinity, and handed down by arch-Angels of the higher worlds to any man who is not afraid of wisdom.

I have penetrated the barrier of invisibility through my purity, and lack of fear, by telepathic communication and astral meditation. God is my true protector, and I am his servant, the true Godman and the grandson of wisdom. Wisdom is my true name, so any man seeking wisdom is seeking me as well.

The Two Rings of the Higher Worlds

The two rings of the spiritual reality needs some explaining. Both rings are given to the novice by the higher forces of the higher worlds. The ring of protection is the ring given by God and serves as a protection against the evil forces, and represents a Halo. The other ring which is called the ring of confidence is given by the Devil, to symbolise one's courage in the world of darkness which is controlled by him, and is called the plane of lost souls, and is the plane that mediums communicate with, to evoke the dead.

The highest world of the higher worlds is controlled by the God of purity and wisdom, and is called the light world.

A mathematical hypothesis proving God's or ALLAH's existence in his invisibility by using a physical example to the point of abstraction. To demonstrate and substantiate God's existence in his invisibility by simply using the fractional divisions of a ruler to prove this theory by a simple analogous exercise.

Formula 2X	16	1 = 8/8	Formula /2
	32	1/2 = 4/8	
	64	1/4 = 2/8	
	128	1/8 = 2/16	
	256	1/16 = 2/32	
	512	1/32 = 2/64	
Point of Invisibility	1024	1/64 = 2/128	
or	2048	1/128 = 2/256	
Abstraction	4096	1/256 = 2/512	
	8192	1/512 = 2/1024	Point of Invisibility
	16384	1/1024 = 2/2048	
	32668		
	65336		
	130672		
	261344		
	532688		
	1065376		
	2130752		
	4261504		
	8523008		
	19046016		
	38092032		
	76184064		
Infinite and Incomprehensible	152368128	Parts of an 1"	

Transmigration by Evolution, of Lighter Spirits

The transmigration of souls through evolution goes through a process of weightlessness in the cleansing chamber of the column of evolution. They are purified to a hundred million degrees light air or spirits, so that the upper gravity of evolution, equivalent to God, assists the souls or purified light air on their way to the planes of their purity. The souls or spirits, before their release from the death cycle here that leads to hell, go through this process of purification, washing away the heavy properties of air or sin, activating a consciousness of light, ascending the spiritual straight of evolution, and becoming infinite with God and wisdom, which the Devil is completely unaware of, plunging deeper in to darkness, back into solidified matter, to be lost in its abyss, with his army of lost souls never to be animated again. So cleansing the soul is inevitable for slipping over to the spiritual straight to God and paradise, for the lost souls are the waste of evolution.

The Spirit Occupancy of the Body

The spirit during the time that it occupies the body, needs to be developed to its full capacity, for the spirit departs from the body with the amount of information, spiritual as well as historically comprehended by it during its occupancy of the body, and a spirit that is not awoken spiritually is completely lost, and directed to the plane of lost souls, after its departure from the body by the principle of the spiritual reality. For without the brain of the body, which is a receptacle for information, received from the higher worlds, the spirit is unable to continue its development, until its re-entry into a new body here on earth, and this development can only be achieved by mysticism, which is a combination of metaphysics, ontology, dialectic, philosophy, and all the true sciences (which assist the development of the five other levels of perception of the soul) and are fundamental to spiritual science, and are based on the divine laws of God.

Perception of Ideas

Ideas are perceived in the cosmic chamber of the brain and transmitted to the mind, which serves as a camera to capture the abstract form of the object from the spiritual reality, which is controlled by the two forces, one of the higher world and the other of the lower world. So in fact the mind is only a receptacle for the ideas which come from without, and once we leave ourselves clear of activities of a physical nature and direct our thoughts to the understanding of the universe, telepathic communication begins with the two forces in the form of materialistic or spiritualistic revelations. If we apply ourselves to the former revelation, the end product, results in an invention of two categories, animate and inanimate, divided into classes of dangerous or beneficial, and the criterion for their acceptance is their utility, however catastrophic these inventions may be when used (in the dangerous class) for the purpose of wars, dominance, and the destruction of mankind. In the beneficial class, the criterion is their domestic function and commercial value which is destined to have a psychological effect on the public, which plunges into debt to the benefit of the capitalist. If we apply ourselves to the later revelation, the end product falls into two categories of pure and impure, divided into classes of art and literature, and moral and immoral. The pure comes from the God of love and understanding, the impure from the false God of hate and destruction. So the inventions that are of a destructive quality and the literature that is of a corrupt quality are closely related, and belong to the lower world of knowledge, and the invention, art, and the literature that are pure come from the higher world of wisdom, which many men have failed to ascend to, because they lack the purity that is necessary as a key to this domain.

There is no paradox
In mysticism,
Only reality.

In the Name of God, Most Gracious, Most Merciful

The Origin of Our Problems

The present economic world problems and natural phenomena which are confronting mankind cannot be solved as many of us would like to think, by simply introducing policies of a national superficial flavour. This sort of action is surely just treating the disease and ignoring the cause, which could be traced as far back to the initial stages of our democratic philosophies and economic ideals. Throughout our history we have been only concerned with our democratic freedom and the animalistic expediency of survival of the fittest, both national and in foreign affairs; this of course applies to all nationals of the world.

We claim to have developed the art of shrewdness in dealing with our neighbours at home and abroad, defending what we believe to be our God-given right (but how wrong we are) and ignoring theirs. These are just some of the phases that form the basis of our reasoning. Good names are for fools. The wise must live off the foolish. Survival of the fittest. The strong must dominate the weak. If he's down, keep him down. Money is God. To be kind is to be stupid. If he's black keep him back, and we agree to disagree. We agree to differ in opinions. With these sayings now intrinsic in the individual, political parties, and the governments of the world, justice becomes null and void, understanding and reason give away to opposition. Which brings us again to the present economic crisis facing this nation. All three political parties agree that the country must be united if inflation is to be curbed but drastically disagree about getting together to work out a solution, because of their different schools of thought. This is one of the reasons why many of the internal problems are left unresolved, not to mention the injustice which motivates their policies, but here you have the leaders exercising their parliamentary democratic right to differ in opinion to the nation's distress. (So much for democracy.) We may say so what, but if we are honest in our examination of the world's problems, we shall see clearly their origins, just as democratic negligence gave birth to unionism. As a protective means of the wage earner, we are told that this valuable guardian of the truly hard-working wage earner is a threat to our society and an ally to communism. But the threat lies in our injustices, falsehood, inconsideration, treachery, deceit, and false reasoning, so clearly our problems are psychological, which makes it impossible for any of our policies to work for very long, without creating some other problem. This fact is apparent in all our endeavours, to name a few, our politics, technology and medicine. I am very surprised that our professional psychologists and criminologists have not traced our citizens' complex dualistic behavioural patterns to the systems which cultivate them. Conventional means can no longer solve our problems, or save our beloved democracy, nor could communism be a substitute for the healing of our democratic ailment. The only panacea, and I stress this most emphatically, is drastic change to a more humanist system with stronger overtures to Godism. Which calls for a spiritual realisation.

Natural Phenomena

The European influence which we exported to the rest of the world by force, during our colonial aggression, disrupting the indigenous, religious and cultural systems of others and substituting our alien philosophies for our economic gain, is now severely felt, and rightly so, for what could be more absurd than a people giving up their mystic teaching and adhering to a philosophy of an inferior nature? Thus the repercussions are famine, drought, earthquakes, and tornadoes, as can be seen in India, Africa, and South America, shortage of grain in Russia, and our world-wide economic crisis. But these things are only the beginning of our sorrow, as said by Christ (Matthew, Chapter 24).

The Foundations of our Societies

The foundations of our societies were laid down by great short-sighted philosophers, who pursued the physical side of nature, completely forgetting, or rather not knowing anything about, the spiritual side of nature, which is far more important to mankind. If mankind is ever to become a responsible creation as intended by his Creator, we have only to direct our thoughts to the situations of the world and we shall see very clearly where these so-called great thinkers' conclusions have led us. They gave us materialism as the dominating factor hitherto, the repercussions of which we are facing at the present. If after all these years man's only desire is to destroy himself, it becomes apparent that he is still in his infancy and is showing no sign of ever growing up into the responsible being that he could, or should, be, but will never be, as long as he continues to cogitate in the physical reality. He has to realise that his physical actions are reflections of his soul and from these reflections we could deduce the terrible state his soul is in.

Now, how could souls in this terrible condition ever hope to enter the Kingdom of God without first being purified? Where is the civilisation that the supposed leaders of mankind continue to speak of? Where is the progress they keep saying we have made? Judging from mankind's uncivilised conduct and values, I would regard these statements as a misconception. The leaders of mankind, past and present, spoke of, and are speaking on and on about a higher standard of living and our achievements in technology. But still there is no change in man himself and he is deteriorating faster than a piece of ice in the tropical sun.

What, we might well ask, is wrong with man that he finds it so impossibly hard to live in peace with his fellow man? He will argue that he has made progress, and to some extent this is true, when viewed from a physical reality, but this same progress has created in our lives a tangle of confusion. Do our leaders really want peace, or is the word peace just another word in their vocabulary? I haven't noticed one instance in all the summit meetings that took place between the so-called great powers of the world that conveyed any such notion. Am I honestly to believe that these myopic Presidents and Premiers of the world truly care about mankind? What could be more ludicrous than the recent display in the year of our Lord 1986, when both the American and Russian representatives failed to reach an agreement to rid the world of the paranoia it's living in, because they could not bring themselves to compromise on humanity's behalf? When such callousness as displayed and by such leaders is given priority over nuclear disarmament, it becomes clear that humanity is of no importance to such men. The world leaders and their advisors have departed from the true path of life, and certainly have strayed from the galaxy of man.

The Moral Ethic

The moral ethic of both communism and democracy implies, when analysed without prejudice, that morality and humanity are absent, and that the residue of the two systems can be defined as corruption, dominance and interference. In all of life's history, never have two systems claimed such authenticity for the governing of races of people whose very souls they try most desperately to destroy, at the price of military aid coupled with a deteriorating morality by death technicians and vegetating soldiers, while at the same time, holding these countries and people to economic ransom. When we look at Africa, here we see a very old people, whom the Heavenly Father blessed with wealth, transforming themselves into western tyrants with each waking day. This gives a good picture of democracy. When we look from Africa across to the East we see communism, which appears like the reflection of democracy. But we must not be fooled by these systems' façades.

As a spiritualist, I have looked into the core of these two systems to ascertain the nature of the spirits which motivate them, and after great scientific pursuance in the spiritual reality my findings gave me the authority to state frankly that the Devil was solely responsible for these two systems. The only difference in the two systems is that where communism rejects God, having a very slight humanist element in its structure, democracy pretends to accept God, but fails to put into practice the theocratic principle, which conveys a spiritual similarity. The destruction of man could be the sole outcome, if these two systems are allowed to survive.

Man has got to take a spiritual telescopic view of the world, if he wishes to see clearly where he's going. By this I mean he has got to view the world through the eyes of His creator. But to look through this spiritual telescope he has got to purify his soul. In this way he could be united with Allah in the spiritual straight, and so view the world through the eyes of Allah, using his mental faculty to comprehend what he sees, but under the supervision of Allah, as he points out the reasons for our problems.

Any man who truly had this experience would embrace the religion of peace. For as a true mystic he would recognise that revelation helps the individual to live a normal life, conforming to the knowledge that Allah is real and every man sooner or later must meet him. So it's much better to achieve this in this life while there is time to do so, in the pursuit of perfection. The purpose of life here on earth is to prepare ourselves for a place in heaven or the hereafter, for definitely we would not be allowed to take our bad habits there. For a higher sense of morality is practised on these planes and our learning must begin here on this planet, knowing full well how we must behave on our arrival there, for in Heaven full peace and understanding go hand in hand with love and respect for all its inhabitants under Allah's Grace. And man could only have true peace through understanding, which is given by Allah. For left to his own intellect he's limited and contradictory, until the unity with Allah takes place, which helps the development of the five other levels of perception, transcending the level where most of mankind is at present. Therefore a perfect behavioural pattern must be accomplished here to be practised there; many of the people we know here on earth would make our lives a misery in Heaven if they were to arrive there with all their evil ways. That's why they would have to be sent elsewhere, and the perfectee would have the peace he desires. The peace world leaders keep talking about (but cannot achieve) and the ecclesiastics pray for, with no response from Allah, is a sign that they lack the understanding that makes this possible. And it's therefore necessary to repudiate these systems of things and turn to Allah in all earnest as the truth is with Allah not Satan, and the way we live with each other here is our passport to better things in the hereafter. This is called superlative understanding, attained by mystical experience coupled with religious principles, which basic law starts with the Ten Commandments and the teaching of Christ, with full brotherhood in Islam in the system of Godlinism as prescribed in the holy scriptures. The Creator has no desire to deceive us but to help us discover our true character, which is his own in likeness, and his character is divine and so is our own. But this world's systems are so uncharacteristic of him that it becomes clear to the traveller or the seeker on the path of truth, that it's in the hands of the impostor Satan, whose delight it is to manufacture conflicting opinions. This is so apparent in every sphere of our lives as we see in politics, philosophy, theology, economics, judiciary, psychology and even among some so-called mystics, but the truth remains the same, and all true travellers receive the same message, which confirms the prophetic message. There is also the reward of many other enlightenments and delights. And always remember that Allah said, if two or three are gathered in His name, He is always present, and many of the world's gatherings are under some fictitious name and not Allah's. So you see clearly whose supervision they are under, and remember too the pleasures of this world are short-lived. The world needs wisdom and wisdom is with Allah, but the world has divorced itself from Him. Another of man's mistakes is that he shows off to his neighbour, when in a good position, and despises the poor and needy, cultivating class consciousness, another of Satan's doings, which was the cause of his fall from grace.

IN THE NAME OF GOD, MOST MERCIFUL,
MOST GRACIOUS

THE TEN COMMANDMENTS

(1) Thou shall have no other God but me

(2) Thou shall not create any graven image of things in the heavens or under the earth or in the sea

(3) Thou shall not bow down thyself to them, nor serve them: for I the Lord thy God am a jealous God visiting the iniquity of the fathers upon the children unto the third and fourth generation of them that hate me and show mercy unto thousands of them that love me and keep my commandments

(4) Thou shall not take the Lord's name in vain: for the Lord will not hold him guiltless that taketh his name in vain

(5) Honour thy father and thy mother that thy days may be long in the land that God giveth thee

(6) Thou shall not kill

(7) Thou shall not commit adultery

(8) Thou shall not steal

(9) Thou shall not bear false witness against thy neighbour

(10) Thou shall not covet thy neighbour's house nor wife nor his man servant or his maid servant nor his ox nor his ass (nor his car) nor anything that is his

Originally the Fifth commandment: Remember the Sabbath day to keep it holy?

To walk with God is to see clearly where one is going.
Brahmam

Dr Spirit . . . .

And Evolving Soul

A soul filled with wrong information delays its development, whilst causing the person concerned a tremendous amount of ill health, and with a lack of knowledge by the person concerned, he or she is unable to comprehend the divine consciousness in relation to the higher levels of perception. Wrong information is induced into you from the type of books you read, and this begins quite early in your education, subjugating the soul and making you submissive to doctrines that were reached by the complexities of sophistry of man's own imagination due to their atheism, which deters and corrupts the soul. And unfortunately you are unable to question them, due to the fact of their higher levels of perception, which is only two levels higher than the level which you are functioning at. But the soul's evolution starts with its own dissatisfaction, resulting in a desire to know the truth (while other persons are guided by Allah in his mercy) and from this instance begins to evolve, coming out gradually from the darkness that men have been living in ever since they rejected the Laws of God and decided on the substitution of their own laws, which was inspired by the devil, and a delight it was for him. The world at present is going through a state of dissatisfaction and especially among the younger generation, due to the false indoctrination which they are beginning to recognise. Truth is very badly needed in the west, to guide these souls to enlightenment. (These souls are labelled as "trouble makers"; and as people who are unable to cope with life.) And the lack of knowledge of the evolutionary process activates a dual personality in the person in a desire to know Allah, although still under the control of the devil. (Those people who are in unison with the devil never suffer dualism.) In such cases like this, the person is now under the influence of the two spirits of the higher world, but one of the spirits is the impostor the devil, who continues his deception in his pretence to be God, in severe cases causing the person to do many evil things in God's name. The other spirit is the true deity Allah spoke of in the Holy Bible and the glorious Koran, the deity of 'Noah Abraham Isaac Jacob' Christ and Mohammed peace be upon Them all, and is alive today as he was from the beginning of time, and I should know because I myself have had his guidance and have been afflicted for several years in the past. This wonderful and divine, majestic and generous being is constantly looking over us, without us knowing, and is very concerned about you, but your only chance of getting to know him is on the spiritual path of mysticism, which every dissatisfied soul is truly seeking. Your soul in this state could never be satisfied in this society we have today. Your soul needs its nourishment and if given the wrong one, it would become dormant, making a cabbage of you or making you physically active, but mentally incapable of thinking for yourself, or you could go down the road of the psychopath.

A person who has read widely stores a considerable amount of information, speaking at great length very impressively, but not doing any thinking of his own, on the very subject he's speaking on. You'll find this type of information soul-destroying, which brings us to the situation we are faced with today. You may think as a special individual you are not included in this devastating wasting away of soul, but you are, and this also applies to the people who control your life. You, if you don't know, would readily say so, but the people who are in control will never admit they don't, but would pretend to do so, and conjure up false information, which is damaging to your soul's development. And here is where spiritual guidance is truly needed in your life, which the western world has been completely devoid of and permanently stagnated. Now that we have reached this point, read carefully what I am saying to you. These two spirits controls our lives: the Holy Spirit which is Allah the creator and sustainer of the universe, the giver and the taker of life to whom we have to give account for how we live our lives. The Evil Spirit is Satan the devil, the great impostor whose sole endeavour is to mislead mankind and to prove to our creator man's ingratitude to him, and to deprive mankind of paradise by his deception, which he is very clever at. It is said of him in the Holy Koran that he is the sworn enemy of man. One has to learn to recognise the attitudes and characteristics of the two spirits, and exorcise the impostor by getting to know your creator better, by observing His laws as a seeker of truth. Then the evil impostor, who was educated into you by your educator, who is his main advocate, would have to vacate allowing the Holy Spirit to take its rightful place in your life.

The evil spirit became very helpful to the constructors of this system when the state and church went their separate ways with both institutions deteriorating to their present levels of obscurity and stagnation in the pursuit of their own interest, neglecting what was best for mankind. The Holy Spirit is likewise helpful, when any person decides to do good, in spite of a continued interference from the evil spirit, who tries to prevent you in your effort. But if you persevere in your endeavour, the Holy Spirit will see you through, but the Holy Spirit would never force you to do what you don't want to do even though He's your creator, but the evil spirit would. The evil spirit is easily recognisable in the physical reality where he uses one of his advocates to try and stop you, for some selfish reason of his or her own, when in fact they are doing the evil spirit's dirty work. Another good example of the evil spirit at work is when you are having an intelligent discussion with a friend or anyone that you might meet, when suddenly out of nowhere one of his advocates just appears, and becomes cleverly involved in the discussion, interrupting the smooth trend of the discussion with his opposition and trying to impress those present to boost his or her ego and divert attention from the true course of the discussion (democratically acceptable but spiritually devastating). When this happens you should tell the person concerned that he or she has got the devil in them. The person will then react in either of these ways: become more aggressive, very quiet or leave, as soon as they are recognised. But if you don't, they will prevent you from reaching an understanding of the truth of the matter discussed. If at any time this should happen to you when used by the devil as his advocate unknown to yourself, don't be upset because it is better to be told the truth and do something about it (for the devil sometimes uses seekers who are not yet clear in their reasoning to do his dirty work). For saving your soul, which is housed in the body (and so very precious), is most important. Judgement day will soon come and it is how you live your life in the here and now that will determine your fate in the hereafter, when that day comes. It is advisable that you should start taking an interest in the spiritual side of life if you wish to attain salvation as promised by our creator.

By now you will have gathered how damaging false information is to your soul, and how important it is to know the truth about life and how it should be lived. This truth, when it is found, is referred to in Buddhism as Nirvana, and is the stage where one is no longer under the law of Karma and now begins to enjoy the fruits of Rama, which in mysticism means heavenly bliss, that all the true devotees of Islam enjoy, being aware of Allah's presence and enjoying his company and becoming his devotee, and so receiving the holy spiritual benefit and full evolution of the soul and release from the devil and the death cycle.

The true Islamic faith means total surrender to the creator of one's life in its entirety for one's release from the death cycle. To fall short of this understanding is to delay one's spiritual development. Submission in prayer (without adoration), beseeching him for material things and the four other pillars of Islam, if practised, assure the believer that his good and bad deeds will be weighed in the balance to decide his or her fate on judgement day.

The chart on the right is better known as the spiritual tree of life in mysticism. It shows the evolutionary level of perception of the soul as it begins to evolve to its full being, which releases it from the animal level which man has descended to, the human level, and on to the higher state of the Godly being.

THE WAY TO GOD AND FUTURE HAPPINESS

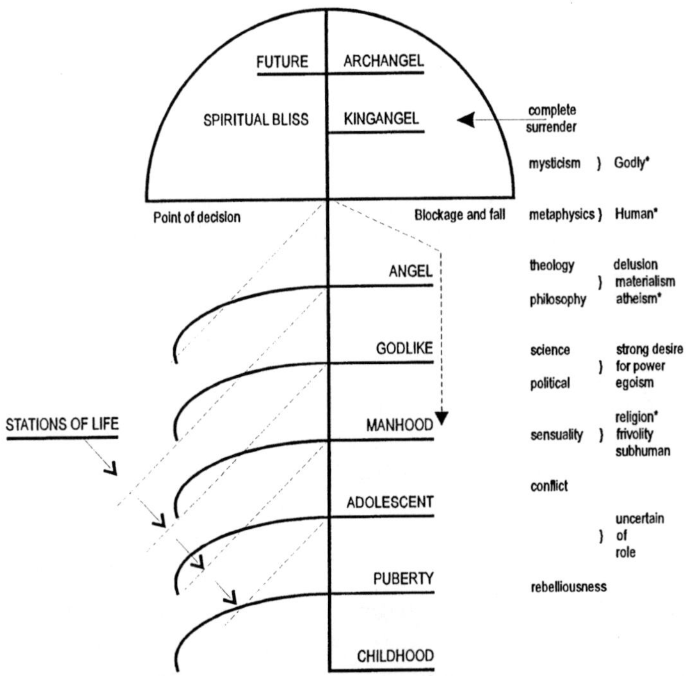

(1) Broken lines on left side signify graduation in man's life.
(2) Curved lines signify spiritual falls and depression.
(3) Short solid lines on right side signify perception and dispositions.
(4) Asterisks to far right show stages of man's development.

The spiritual tree of life on the path of Truth.

It is imperative for the world to make a right-about-turn to the path of truth, understanding and peace and true religion, for to pray and talk of peace and love all at the same time, ignoring the commandments, is hypocritical, for the civil laws of God must be implemented in one's life before one could hope to ascend to the higher religious obligation (of the true believer) which leads to perfection, as ordained by the Creator, and that will bring peace to the world.

Righteous Warrior.

The Attainment of Spiritual Enlightenment

The attainment of spiritual enlightenment can only be achieved by examination of oneself and one's behaviour, and by correcting one's bad habits as one detects or realises them floating to the surface of the mind's eye, repenting to God and asking for forgiveness for one's many wrong doings, and truly making amendment for one's ways as one travels on the spiritual road of peace and life and total surrender to God. For it is only when a man surrenders completely to God that he can truly accomplish his endeavour on the spiritual road.

Let any man observe the Ten Commandments and he will see the result, for they are the basic laws that were given to man by God to guide him to the spiritual road. Every religion comprises these ten laws in its moral code, but they are referred to by different names in the various religious orders, conveying to man the same advice of abstinence from the things that are detrimental to him, and helping the individual to acquire the ability to reason, without distortion, between what is right and what is wrong, and bringing him closer to God and His supreme plan.

God is concerned with the soul of man, not with his body. The body soon will die, but the soul lives on, and the state the soul lives in after death depends on the person's disposition here on earth. This is the reason why God keeps on warning mankind through the ages by Covenants and Messengers, who beseech mankind relentlessly to cleanse their souls through repentance, Zakat or Alms and Prayers. These three media, when put into practice, elevate man's spiritual self and help him to become self-realised and more aware of his weak position in a world full of forces, invisible as well as visible, with which he has to contend, knowingly or unknowingly during the course of life.

Of course the body is an important vessel, maintained by the physical necessities such as sunlight, air, water and vegetation, unceasingly given to man and withdrawn from him only when he is punished for his national sin. And as his body becomes weak with the absence of these four necessities, so likewise the three media mentioned above strengthen his soul, being in closer communion with its creator. (Such souls are truly peaceful souls and receive constant favours from God.) Man is a spiritual being; his true source of life is in the spiritual world and his endeavours should be in this direction. How can I convey to man what it is like to meet God and how important it is for one to cleanse oneself of all the impurities that one accumulates during one's life time? God has visionary language which He uses for speaking to man, sleeping or awake, giving man some indication of His presence, but this seems to be ignored or misinterpreted by man, either by his blindness or ignorance, and for this reason man is forever lost in the physical state of life, drifting further away from God and into scientific disaster. Man has become a worshipper of nuclear science. He feels that science is going to solve all his problems, but can science help the soul in perdition? Mankind's detachment from God and attachment to science is ludicrous. This to me is like a child giving up his parents and clinging desperately to the medical staff who were present at its birth, oblivious of its parents. And what would be the parents' reaction to such behaviour? They being the first cause, would they blame themselves for going wrong somewhere, or accuse the child of being ungrateful, or condemn the medical staff for the helping hand they gave? And what measure would they take to bring an end to such a situation? This is the situation that God found Himself in with the people of Noah, and he had to destroy the inhabitants for turning away from him, for worshipping idols, and for their perversion. In our time it shall be for science and its perversion, as prophesied in the Holy Scriptures, and most of mankind shall perish, for most of mankind bluntly refuse to accept the spiritual truth, which is tangible to anyone or any nation who cares to know it and put its recommended laws into practice.

See Sura XL 82 - 85.

When will man realise the damage philosophy has caused as compared to mysticism, which is its sister science, but, of course, at a much higher level on the path of truth that leads us to God and spiritual development. The acceptance of a mundane philosophy as the criterion of life, and the rejection of the mystical messages of God, has brought about this catastrophic world situation, which men of very small minds are trying to solve by the science of philosophies which were handed down from generation to generation to this present day, completely disregarding the Laws of God (which are intended for the betterment of mankind), and clinging foolishly to the sophist doctrines which have gotten mankind into this state of confusion and which they are foolishly trying to accept as normality, but is it? Some people would argue that we are living in the age of science and therefore have no need for God, as though science could ever replace God in our lives. But have they ever stopped to think that God is the creator of the phenomena of science, and no science, whether good or evil, could function without His sole power, which is seen and yet not recognised. The argument now will be: if God's sole power is the energy of the phenomena of science, why hasn't God withdrawn this energy, so crippling man's pursuits in this direction? The answer to this is quite simple: God has given man a choice between what is good and what is evil, and laws of wisdom to observe, and if they are observed He will always help man make the right decision in matters concerning his welfare. I wonder if the leaders of mankind are aware of this truth. I wonder if the philosophical writers of today are aware of this truth. I wonder if the theologians are aware of this truth. Should they claim that they are aware of this truth, then where is the implementation of the laws of wisdom? Which leads us to these further questions: why is the world so confused? Why is the world so chaotic? Why is the world so painful? Why is the world so unruly? Why is the world so sinful? Why is the world in such darkness? Could these important questions be answered by science, which man has now accepted as his God? As for the leaders of mankind, would they confess to the world that they are egotistic and power mad, and not really in a position to solve these problems, whether scientifically, economically, politically or industrially, as these problems were inherited by them, although created by their predecessors, who opposed the laws of God in the age of ignorance, substituting the Devil's philosophies in their place, so causing man to fall into a pit of darkness and spiritually lose his way?

Let every true believer pray these recommended prayers daily:

Psalm 140 from the Holy Bible or Torat and Sura CXIII from the Holy Quran so that they may be saved from this treacherous plan of Satan.

Mankind has taken two of the greatest books ever written and philosophised their true meaning away. In the Western world the intellectuals and theologians, speaking of the lyrical verses of the Holy Bible instead of its meaning, using a million words to describe its beauty, hold it as one of the greatest masterpieces ever written, yet completely ignore its guidance and laws and bring Christianity to a halt. In addition to this Western folly I have heard it said that no one could truly understand the Holy Quran and that it needs years of studying. Isn't one thousand five hundred years an ample period of time to comprehend its meaning? Would God give man two books beyond man's capacity? In the Middle East and Eastern Asia the philosophical atmosphere is different; the argument is, there is no God but Allah, and Mohammed is His prophet and the Holy Quran cannot be translated into another language, for it loses its phonetical beauty, but does it lose its meaning? To me the meaning is quite clear and simple. Show me where a true Islamic or Christian Government exists in the world at present. Do not both Muslims and Christians realise that instead of arguing about their prophets, who brought the same message of repentance to mankind, they should be giving guidance to mankind instead of being subordinates to the Devil's establishment? From Adam's time to this day the Lord has given us one faith to adhere to, and this faith depends on total surrender of ourselves to God, which leads us to Islam, but true Islam (Sura LIV 17, 22, 32, 40, 47).

If the unspiritual brothers of faith hate me for speaking the truth, then may Allah have mercy on their souls, but if they come out from behind the veil of darkness behind which they are hidden, and surrender themselves to Allah and acknowledge the truth, may Allah's blessing be upon them.

Religious Leadership, Administration and the World Problems

Most of the world's social, political and economic problems could have been avoided had the world's religion been totally understood by those responsible for its propagation. Clearly the purpose of religious doctrine was meant to elevate the souls of men, so that they would eventually establish just societies and stable governments, which leads to salvation.

Governments should govern by the divine laws, which every minister of the government must also adhere to, for what is the duty of government if not to guide and be the guardian of the people under its responsibility? And this responsibility should be held in reverence, we are told by men of a pious disposition, who by their very nature are most susceptible to divine instruction.

Their public and private lives never differ from the religious laws that permeate and shape the society's behaviour as a whole, for they know any deviation from the divine law, for whatever purpose or reason, must inevitably lead to abnormality and a miscarriage of justice, which would doubtlessly lead the governed to suspicion, distrust, and disrespect of the minister of the government, and more damaging than this, would bring the religion itself wrongly into disrepute, by members of society who have no knowledge of the religious laws, and so judge the religion by its administrators, who fall short of their responsibility as good shepherds.

In this respect, both the Islamic and democratic world stand out like a sore thumb, in a time when the world truly needs leadership. Recently, there has been public punishment of offenders of the Law, as was recommended in our Law. But what about the other aspect of the Islamic teaching which makes up the moral codes and which must be adhered to, especially by those who are entrusted with the responsibility of administration? Are these moral codes to be ignored? And broken by those in authority? And not result in serious repercussions for the nation, as we see in the Western world today, where atheists' movements and their subordinates are organising themselves against the believers, whom the Message of Islam is supposed to be for? Aren't these the type of leaders and followers who are mentioned in the Holy Quran Sura XXXVIII - 60 - 61?

The followers shall cry to the misleaders: "Nay, ye too! No welcome for you! It is ye who have brought this upon us! How evil is this place to stay in!"

They will say: "Our Lord! Whoever brought this upon us, add to him double penalty in the fire."

And they would say: "Our Lord! We obeyed our chiefs and our Great one and they misled us as to the right path."

The passage makes it quite clear to us Muslims whom we should follow and whom we should not, and therefore we must be in a position to judge the actions of those who lead us in times like these.

Reform is now necessary of the concept of what government is for. Islamic Leaders and administrators must now decide whether their role, apart from adjudication, is to oppress or to care for those they are in charge of, not a very difficult dilemma for the righteous men to decide upon, but decide upon it they must, and if the decision they make is in the right direction it would give scope to their thinking and assist the men of learning to come nearer the Prophets' behaviour as administrators and put right the wrongs of their predecessors, who have misguided mankind in the past, and as our contemporaries are doing at the present, which is a catastrophe.

Only the full comprehension and implementation of the concept of Islam, which is an embodiment of all the religious messages sent to man, whose shortcomings are the same the world over, and who is becoming very similar to the days of Noah, can save man. It is now vitally important that these Religious Figures must come together to examine, re-read and comprehend, and then with impartiality unite the believers of the world in the spirit of the Brotherhood of man.

It is no good waving the Holy Books at each other, while the world's believers cry out for guidance and are deceived by the advocates of Satan. The religious message is for the believers, and they await the message with great anxiety. The guardians of this message must now present it to those who await it, without further delay or otherwise they shall forfeit the responsibility of their office.

The Muslim and every thinking man has a responsibility to the poor of the world, but especially the Muslim administrators. The rich politician and wealthy businessman may be currently contributing to the armed struggle, but there is also a great need to feed and clothe the destitute of the world, for they shall bear witness against those who speak of Islam, yet fail to implement its teaching in a practical form.

See Sura LXX 17, 18, 24, 33.

What wonderful opportunities there are in the world today for the manifestation of Islam in its true glory, and why are the Leaders and administrators missing these opportunities, floundering in their dichotomy, what is wrong with the nation (umma) of Islam? Is not Allah Subhana Wata Allah its Divine Head? Or have the nationals decided to pursue the path of the people of the book and lose the Grace of their Creator, for it is said in Sura XXXVIII Verse 82:

(Iblis) said: Then by thy power I will put them in the wrong, except thy servant amongst them, sincere and purified by thy Grace.

So from this floundering of the leaders, we should conclude that they are in the hands of Satan and should take heed of this warning and return to Allah and the truth of their faith.

Never before in history have so many people become so disenchanted with their religious leaders as the Muslim are today with their Imam, for they are not in touch really with their brothers in faith, who have become mature over the years and want true leadership from those who stand before them, preaching about things that all committed Muslims have already rectified in their lives.

The Imams must realise that men who come to the Mosque for Jumah Prayer in times like these need to be treated like men and not like little boys in school. They want to see Islam on the move, and so expect their Imam to be more inspiring.

Who wants to attend Jumah in high spirits and expectation, and leave in low spirits? Shouldn't the Mosque be a place for energising one's soul and strengthening the faith of each other whenever we meet, and so fortifying each brother's spirit to deal with the evil environment that he finds himself in? Instead, what happens is his energy is sapped out of him by the very person who supposedly should stimulate him.

They must also remember that partiality is recognisable by those of us who read the Scripture and that only impartial commentaries must be made, or they will indicate that even in their religion there's one interpretation of Law for the poor, and one for the rich, which is truly an abomination in the eyes of the Lord, and will result in severe punishment on judgement day for those who practice this misguided nepotism.

PHENOMENA OF SELF-INFLECTION ON MANKIND OR PRINCIPLE OF KARMA

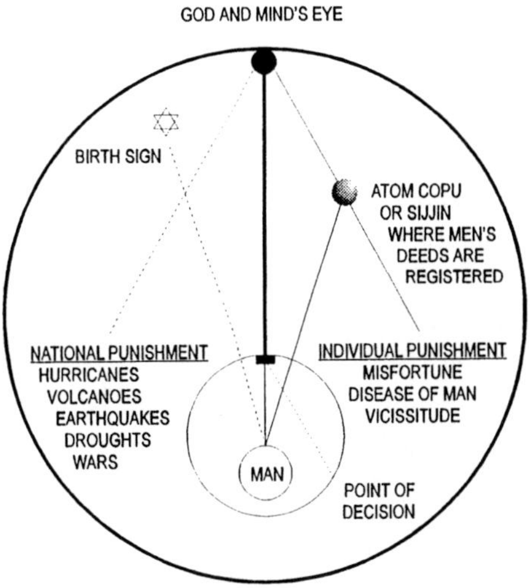

Sura XLII-30:
Whatever misfortune happens to you, is because of the things your hands have wrought, and for many (of them) He grants forgiveness.
Sura LXXXIII:
(7) Nay! Surely the record of the wicked is preserved in Sijjin.
(8) And what will explain to thee what Sijjin is?
(9) (There is) a register (fully) inscribed.

The Truth of Opposition and Division

Many people have asked me what is the truth, and they could be very hostile when they do.

My answer to this question is this, that there are many truths, but there is a main and major truth, and that's the important truth. And they would argue that no such truth exists before inquiring what this truth is. Before we go into this major truth, we shall examine the truth of opposites to see where it leads us, starting with temperature. It is either hot or cold, warm or cool. Next our physical structure: we are either tall or short, big or small, fat or thin, but this is the ordinary truth of opposites which every intelligent person accepts. When we arrive at the abstract truth of opposites, such as false and true, belief or disbelief, good or evil, the conflict begins. God and the Devil are the ultimate of the argument of opposites, which relates to all the other opposites which affect the characteristics of our lives. For example, honesty and dishonesty are related to good and evil, righteousness and ignominy to belief and disbelief etc.

The disbeliever completely disregards the opposites of God and the Devil, and would attack the believer for believing, while maintaining his disbelief, which is the opposite of belief. This brings us to the major truth in which we are interested, the reality of our existence, or the existence of the reality of being, and whichever way we choose to look at it, this remains a major truth, and so, when a man argues that there is no major truth, he is doubting the reality of his being, a rather peculiar thing, for such a person is unaware of his existence. And if he is unaware of being, then he must be in a state of somnambulism, going through life in a dream state, which is very dangerous.

The process of physical evolution is the creative ordinance of our Supreme Lord and applies also to the spiritual evolution of the soul.

Evolution, if it is non-created, must be non-existence and therefore a false theory of the active dreamer. For the universe is the creation of the Supreme phenomenon God, and we are his creation. Nevertheless the Biblical truth confirmed by the Koranic truth and the opposing Darwin's theory of evolution have further divided the world into two categories of people, the creationist and the evolutionist. The evolutionist as we know is a non-believer like his communist counterpart, although he claims to hold democratic political ideals, and could be Conservative, Socialist or Liberal in his thinking. The humanist is also a non-believer, for he rejects God like his evolutionist and communist counterparts. They despise each other, yet they have a very important factor in common, their disbelief.

How, I ask myself, could the creationist hold the same political views as the evolutionist and remain a believer, unless he is being deceptive to himself and others? Another question which arises is whether the humanist and the evolutionist are one and the same person, for democratic though they are, they jointly pose a dangerous threat to the elevation of humanity, as they share the same non-existence idea of God as the communist. So clearly the communist, humanist, evolutionist, naturist and the atheist are one and the same and employ the same motivating force, which hides very cleverly in the divisions of their political ideals of Conservatism, Liberalism, Nationalism and Socialism, democratic yet also communist.

And this divisible disbelief manifests itself again in the materialistic philosophy of both communism and democracy in the desire to share equally in the former, but in a strong refusal to do so in the latter, which creates opposition between East and West, also the conflicts within the democratic system amongst the political parties, who jointly oppose the same force as seen in its communist façade. However, the politically minded person evolves gradually through the various parties of the democratic system to become humanist, which the communist happens to be, for he is slightly less animalistic than his counterpart, the democrat. This force continues to be the Lord of Man.

Politically, the creationist could never be a true democrat, for time and time again he sees the consensus of the majority being wrong in their selection of the government, with which they soon become disenchanted. History bears witness to this fact. And how on earth could these different ideals merge to form one functional whole acceptable to all without conflicts and confusion? Yet all of these ideals are the product of one evil force, that of the Devil or Satan.

As a reminder, here are the divisions again. Take belief first, as one's belief helps to shape one's character. Then the evolutionist, the naturist, the humanist and the creationist, who are further divided by their political ideals of Conservatism, Socialism, Liberalism and Nationalism. But the problem of division does not stop here. It creeps into the religious lives of the democratic people in the form of Catholicism, Pentecostalism, The Baptist Creed, The Jehovah Witnesses, The Seventh Day Adventists, The Quakers, The Mormons, The Church of England and The Rosicrucians, all proposing Christianity but divided in their ideas of what Christianity really is (and this is only the national structure of the western democratic societies).

This further division of the people, in any sensible person's assessment, could mean only one thing: chaos. But in spite of these divisions and differences, they all have one thing in common, and that's selfishness, with its manifold clichés. For example, survival of the fittest, dog eats dog, if he's down keep him down, the strong must live off the weak, the wise must live off the foolish, I'm all right Jack, attitudes which graduate into deceit, treachery, connivance, covetousness, and unconcern for each other, to mention but a few, attitudes which are now intrinsic in the democratic man. And how on earth could these multiple sub-animalistic behavioural patterns bring about the harmony for an acceptable life style that would be beneficial to all? And how could these attitudes they indulge in be ascribed to God? Which leads me to ask this question: Is this what Christianity implies? As far as I'm aware, Christ's teaching is the opposite, so obviously this type of attitude is motivated by the Devil and not God. For would God divide his own house, knowing full well that it would lead to destruction?

We also see the same divisions between the world's major religions; they stand apart, but proclaim the same truth. For example, they all speak of the better life, which is an acceptable fact (which I am aware of) but differ on how to obtain salvation in an almost warlike manner, because their advocates misunderstand the very religion they preach. But if one examines these religions closely, one would recognise their similarity, or oneness, which exists unnoticed by the elites, who poisoned their laymen brothers' minds against each other at the different stages of the same religion that they adhere to for their salvation.

So in fact these religions are the same, and relate to the graduation on the spiritual straight of advancement, and the more spiritually advanced the people of a nation are, the more rigid the discipline, compared to less advanced brothers of the same faith, at a lower run of the graduation ascent. But when a brother of the less rigid discipline departs from this life, if he has applied all the principles required of him, he too, will have salvation, just like his advanced brother of the more rigid discipline at an advanced stage of his faith.

For example, the Buddhist faith requires the seeker who has accepted Buddhism to detach himself from the secular world, so that he can devote all his time to reasoning or meditation, which further him along the spiritual straight to enlightenment and release him from the lower death cycle (which he may never attain in this lifetime, for a simple reason that I will not disclose in this article) onto the plane of his or her purity. But a fact that I should mention here about Buddhism is that when one takes the first step on the spiritual road, one sets off in the pursuit of Nirvana, and so one omits to meet God in one's experience, but nonetheless achieves Nirvana. So true Buddhism is a faith of the higher rung of the spiritual ascent, which can only be practised by the seeker who is truthful to himself, for he takes on himself the full responsibility for his own safety. To keep a clear picture in the mind of the reader of this work, I shall continue to use the name of the religions as known, even though they relate to different stages of the same faith. In Christianity we have the doctrine of the resurrection confirming the Buddhist teaching of liberation from the death cycle to a higher life, indicating that death is not the end, which Christ's ascension to heaven proves and which is later substantiated by proof, but we will come to this later. We also see that like the Buddhist, Christ's Disciples had to give up the secular life to attain their spiritual enlightenment before they could become the representatives of the faith of advanced Judaism. At the same time he told the laymen brothers that all they had to do to be part of this brotherhood was only to believe in him, as believing in him also meant believing in God who sent him, with further instructions about loving thy neighbour as they love themselves. But he gave slightly different instructions to his Disciples when they got agitated about leadership, saying that he who is the greatest among them should serve the others, and, by so doing, administering to the needs of the two groups of people at their different levels. The more rigid disciplines were given to his more responsible Disciples. These simple, but hard to maintain principles have not been practised by the layman, or the so-called spiritual heads, of this time, in our present day society. And although these instructions to the two groups of people were in accordance to their needs, it demanded one thing from them for graduation on the spiritual straight, and that was obedience.

The other advanced religions like Jainism, Krishanism, Taoism, with the exception of Hinduism which holds to polytheism and regards the cow as sacred, maintain the rigid principles, with the Jains sweeping their path as they walk along, trying to prevent killing some tiny creature, though they are often in fact killed by an enthusiastic member of the Jaina Sect, as they are swept out of the way. This is not taken as far in Buddhism. But both are in accordance with the Law.

"Thou shall not Kill", taken to its utmost. A law that Christ himself observed, and advised his followers to follow, but at the same time he warned the people in a parable about a landlord who had a vineyard and let it out and when he sent one of his sons to collect the rents, he was killed. On hearing the news of the death of his son, he sent another of his sons to his tenants, who also killed that son. What, Christ asked, would be the outcome when the father of the two sons comes? The parable was misunderstood then, as it is now, for the landlord that Christ was speaking of was not an ordinary landlord, but God the Creator. But he used the mundane situation to emphasise what the coming of God would be like.

Mohammed, peace be upon him, was given permission to use the sword, similarly Arjana, as we see from the historical events in the Holy Scriptures of the Bhagavad Gita (where our God is known as Lord Krishna, hence the Hari Krishna faith). The rigid discipline requires that everything that one does must be done in the service of the Lord; even the food that one eats must be offered to the Lord first, and then be taken by the devotee, unlike in the religions at the other rung of the same spiritual straight with their covenant of blessing and thanking the Lord for the food he has provided, as in Christianity and Islam, where the disciplines on believers are not as demanding as in Krishnaism. For one waits on the Lord to partake of the food first before he eats it (as a devoted servant would normally do if he was working with a mortal person) which was very much a part of the Mosaic Law and which was the responsibility of the high priest, so maintaining the blessing of God on his people. All these religious rituals correlate to the covenants of advancement or are in accordance to the people's needs in their digression, as in the case of the children of Israel in Christ's time and later in Mohammed's time, Peace be upon them both, when people of the middle eastern countries had fallen to such a low ebb, which brings us to Islam and the last of the Lord's covenant with humanity. Islam is a very gentle but profound faith and requires perseverance and is just the thing for the layman and world leaders today to help them return to, and maintain, a high moral standard, whilst still involved in secular living, as its counterpart Christianity allows, if they are practised. Both Christ and Mohammed emphasise the promise of the resurrection as the main event of man's future, and this depends on his total surrender to Allah, Jehovah or God. Islam has added four other principles to Christ's teachings, which are: praying five times a day, the giving of alms, going to Mecca for Haj (or Pilgrim) and fasting during Ramadan. The first of the tenets is the belief in one God and has been a long established tenet of all the messengers of God.

The application of these five pillars of Islam as they are called, with the omission of the Ten Commandments of the Law of Moses, given to him by God, is to fall short of the Acceptance of the Message of God in its entirety. In fact, what Islam has done is to relieve the malpractising hierarchy of their responsibility to their fellow brothers in faith, and made the individual responsible for himself in the eyes of Allah, under Allah's guidance, yet coming together in a brotherhood, respectful of their Imam, whose life is devoted to the learning of the words of Allah, Subana Wata Allah, as in the Holy Koran and the teaching of the Prophet, Peace be upon him. This teaching must become accessible to every citizen of the Islamic Societies (and the rest of the world) as part of their educational curriculum, for every person of an Islamic state must become a responsible member, likewise Christian Societies of the world, for really Christianity and Islam are one. But Christianity dictated by Rome was motivated by Satanic influences. For don't forget that Satan even tried to persuade Christ to jump from a cliff where he was standing in return for a kingdom here on earth.

Proof of this statement is, for example, the introduction of idolatry into Christianity as part of its ritual and the calling upon the Virgin Mary as an intermediary for man, a position which Christ proclaimed to hold; for he said during the time of his ministry here on earth "he that ask God for anything in my name will receive it". Another thing that's very important in the sayings of Christ is that "no one goes to God except through him". By this, of course, he meant that if one failed to do as he advised, one could not get to God, and this is why very few people have this experience.

And Christ's mother, Bless Her, never said that she was an intermediary; what she said was, "Now that I have given birth to a servant of God, I shall be called blessed among women." She said absolutely nothing about being an intercessor for man. But Roman Catholicism encouraged this misconception and prevented its members from turning to God directly, through the principles of the teaching of Christ, and diverted them to idolatry as a means of salvation, which is forbidden in Holy Scripture. Buddhism also encourages this, but the Buddha himself never indulged in this pagan habit, for he was a truly wise man who had attained enlightenment and would not practice or recommend idolatry, for he practised the higher rung of the faith of detachment, which Christ and Mohammed practised themselves, although they had to achieve this in the midst of their materialistic environment, from which the Buddha became a recluse, as he had everything the world had to offer in his possession, unlike the prophets mentioned above, for they had to refrain from everything the world had to offer them. The same practice of detachment is clearly seen in Jainism and in Krishnaism, which relate to the higher rungs of the same faith, pertaining to the contemplative and impartial reasoning for the evolutionary process of the seeker of enlightenment. We see Christ introducing the reasoning process in the parables he spoke to the people and his Disciples, we see Allah, Subana Wata Allah, in his mercy toward man, in the Holy Koran, beseeching the believer to think of what is said and to contemplate the working of the Universe.

When this process of thinking and reasoning begins, one reaches the threshold of repentance, acquiring forgiveness from God and moving up the spiritual rungs of the ladder to purity and true enlightenment, advanced stages of the same religious path. All prophets and all truly enlightened men know this as one and the same message, which concerns itself with the needs of the people in the most simple form necessary to convey this very important guideline of salvation to man on the lower rungs of the spiritual ladder, who is promised salvation if he believes, but is not released from the process of death and rebirth of the lower death cycle of the planet, until he works to acquire his attainment of detachment from the lower materialistic ideology of the philosophies of the physical reality, which brings out the worst in people, causing them to break and ignore the moral code of life given to us in the Ten Commandments.

For a better relationship with each other in the pursuit of material gains, which is the norm of the societies of the so-called civilised world, we must become detached. The application in our life of the spiritual philosophy of detachment, and the less severe guideline of loving one's neighbours as one loves oneself, as directed by Christ and endorsed by Mohammed (Peace be upon them both) and of loving for your brother, what you love for yourself, would eradicate greed from our lives, for these principles brings out the best in oneself. Now that you have a glimmer of light of the true reality, the physical motivations, the worst in us, and the spiritual, the best, let us go back to the argument of opposites, of the right and wrong ways of life.

Clearly, we can see where the opposites to the right way of life have led us. And the question we have to ask ourselves is whether the world should continue in this devastating direction, and if not, what should be done to change our course, for the choice of a better world is in the hands of the ordinary people, as the leaders of the world have failed most terribly.

We cannot expect to turn away from God who gave us the right way, and serve the Devil, who encourages the wrong way, and still expect happiness in our lives. The Devil, who blinded man from the oneness of his faith, the oneness of the human race, the oneness of his creation, has also segmented governmental bodies of all nations of the earth, creating conflicts, disharmony, dissatisfaction and intolerance. He has caused man to stray so far away from God that if it was not for God's mercy, this world would have been destroyed already, as the people were in the days of Noah, but this delay of destruction is only temporary.

How did we manage to stray so far from the spiritual straight that destruction is now hanging over our lives? Is it our fault or the misguidance of our theologians, philosophers, political leaders and educators for they must be held responsible? Will they refuse to accept the truth now and continue on the road of destruction? They are the ones who claim to be the experts on how we should live our lives, in their deception posing as respectable citizens, when in fact they are the advocates of the Devil, for they never advocate the principles of the Almighty God. In their endeavours, they are more concerned with fame and fortune, the opposite goal of the wise.

The theologians examining the Holy Scriptures of the world store the knowledge of the scriptures, and recite them in parrot fashion, but never apply the principles of the message recommended, and so remain unenlightened and prevent others from achieving this goal, and fall prey to the Devil's influence. That is why the recent message of Islam in its one thousand five hundredth year is a very important message to humanity, for it releases the hierarchy of the religious institutions from their responsibility to us, making every man responsible for himself, since the religious leaders are only concerned with knowledge of the scripture, not the application of the principle of the message, which would help our spiritual growth and so bring about the unification of the divisions of the faith in one spiritual whole in the spirit of divine truth under God.

A fact known to all the messengers of God and all enlightened believers who are united in the true spiritual brotherhood of being.

The divisive force which separate and create conflicts among religious, philosophical, theological and political bodies remain in our educational system. This system was built on sophism (and that is where the origin of our social problem begins) in the philosophical circle of Isocrates, handed down to us by Plato in his works (the most dangerous one being the Republic), where the present day system was engineered. This means Utopia for the ruling classes, geared deliberately to keep the working classes in their place, except of course when they show some intelligence, and become a threat to this Utopia. They are then allowed to become part of the Utopian machinery but, as a subordinate he or she is so overwhelmed by this so-called opportunity that he forgets his salvation and joins the advocates of the Devil in their misdeeds.

The true steps to enlightenment and Islam:- the religion of Peace given to man by Allah through his servants the prophets.

(1) The first thing the sinner and believer must do is to start observing the Ten Commandments of Moses.

(2) The second thing he must do is to examine himself and try to eradicate his faults, as recommended by Christ when he said, "Before you try to take the wart from your brother's eyes, you must first take the plank from your eyes."

(3) Repentance to God for your sins and forgiving others for their wrong-doing towards you.

(4) Total surrender to God, for God alone knows your needs and the way.

(5) Detachment; this is done in a systematic way to ease the pains of detachment from the things one loves. You start by giving up something you treasure most dearly whenever you break the laws or do something which you consider to be stupid.

(6) In your reasoning or examining any subject, be totally impartial. In the watching of any competition remain neutral.

(7) Don't become involved in idle gossip as it belongs to a lower plane, and you are trying to reach the higher planes of understanding and purity.

(8) Read the books that you are guided to intuitively, and not those recommended to you by friends, unless you first had the desire to do so, except of course the Holy Koran, the Bible and The Bhagava Gita and this book.

(9) Don't start on this path if you are a coward and have no intention to continue.

(10) Be fully united with God in Islam and the spiritual straight, for Islam is the faith of our fore-parents, Adam and Eve. All other religions are part and parcel of this path, which is the mystic way to salvation and return from the death cycle of the lower rungs of the spiritual ladder. And this was confirmed by Mohammed, peace be upon him, when he ascended with the Archangel Gabriel through the seven heavens where he saw and spoke to the Holy Ones who had been released from the lower death cycle on his way to see Allah, for his instruction in prayers for the present day Muslim.

(11) Daily prayers.

(12) Giving of alms to the poor and helping the needy in society.

THE
TESTIMONY
OF SADGLAD-ALLAH'
MYSTICAL
EXPERIENCE AND THOUGHTS
IN THE SIXTIES, SEVENTIES
AND EIGHTIES AS WRITTEN
THEN WITH NO CHANGE TO
THE TEXT.

THE
MYSTICAL
PHILOSOPHICAL
POLITICAL
POEMS AND ESSAYS
BY
SADGLAD

HUMBLE SERVANT
OF THE
LORD MOST HIGH.
DR SPIRIT ...

DESIRES

Tis not war I want but peace,
Tis not fame I seek but justice
Tis not negotiation I crave but freedom
Tis not hate I have but love
Tis not sex I yearn for but wisdom
Tis not friends I need but committed believers in faith
Tis not lies I'm after but truth
Tis not man I fear but Allah
I know that you think I'm a fool
But the world is more foolish than I am

URGENT

Give us back our destiny,
Put it in our hands.
Keep your bales of cotton,
Which you yourselves don't understand.
And leave our eyes alone, to watch you in your quandary,
For our minds are no longer yours,
We demand our destiny.

The sooner you comply, tis the better for us all.
For I foresee a raging sea
That may drown us all ...

You fixed your date of independence
For a few black States.
But the time has come to fix the date
For the emancipation of the entire race.

POLITICAL RECIPE

The world is like a pot on fire,
And the cuisine is efficacious,
But the master chefs responsible
Are long since dead and gone.
But their unholy recipe lives on and on,

Hence the concoction for today is "I'm alright right Jack"
Capitalism, and here's the recipe:
Take forty billion pounds of it,
And spread it unevenly around at a board meeting,
Add a handful of Grecian democracy and
Conservative bureaucracy.
Mixing well together in a parliamentary party
Or confrontation bowl,
Pour unevenly on forty years of inflation
And social injustice.

Now mix carefully with some rhetoric,
Manifestos, unemployment, unionism, privatisation,
Delusion, and a pinch of excuses.
Now you've got a nice and confused democratic
Political situation. Put into a universal pot
And boil indefinitely. Add a touch of liberalism, socialism,
Fascism, oh yes some racism too,
Or what ever take your fancy, and consume while hot.
Now drop dead, you deceptors.

RHETORIC

All these rhetorical speeches
Made in parliament
By the country's most treacherous men
Are certainly not getting us any place
But are making a mockery of the populace.

They told us of their plans and policies
For putting right the country's economy,
But so far nothing they said has materialised,
And now they're back at us again,
With a new set of lies.

But that's politics, believe me
When I tell you it's full of tricks.

I remember when they said
There'll be full employment for every man,
Council houses galore, just put up your hands.
But then they came with the squeeze
Backed up by freeze,
That brought the country down to its knees.

But that's politics, believe me
When I tell you it's full of tricks.

And just before they came into power
They convinced most of us
That they had the answer
So we voted wholeheartedly,
And now they have us living in misery.

DEMOCRACY

I am not a man who slanders,
But, democracy, you've done me wrong,
And now I have divorced you
To tread upon new ground.
You stretch your tentacles across the world
As a chronic cancer, you must admit
You made an autopsy necessary,
And now you are in a fit.
Now that we physicians have seen your structure clear,
We intend to operate, without the slightest fear.
Your conditioning has failed with me,
And many such as I.
Democracy, you are a beast,
And don't try to deny,
The poor proletariat work their fingers to the bone
To retire in old age with a TV, and no home.
Work harder, work harder, that's all they ever hear
Trumpeted in their ears from year to year
By the beastly politicians and capitalists
Who really don't care.
Is there no end, can't you hear their cry?
How much longer are you going to turn a blind eye?
It would seem to me, democracy,
You had on heart from your original start,
And the devil has been your light,
Along the democratic path.
Democracy, Democracy, how do you plead?
Not guilty, I suppose, but you can't fool me.

INFLATION

The flames of inflation are burning high,
The nation ignores the politician's cry.
Meanwhile, the chancellor seeks inaccessible remedies
For the economic pains in the deficit sea.
The experts bark unceasingly, By Jove,
Something must be done,
We could influence the Arabs to lend us a hand,
For the pound is under the magician's wand,
Now you see it, now you don't.
With wages scarcely rising, and astronomical pricing,
In conjunction with over-taxing,
And unemployment continually increasing,
Will the church continue sleeping?
The unions, some people say,
Are a threat to the nation, day by day.
But is this really true, for without it, who's
Going to protect me and you?
The question now is, shall we stay in the E.E.C.
Or secede and hold on to our Sovereignty?
For the captain of the ship of promise,
Beseeched us one and all. He said, "Let patience be your motto,
And please help me through this storm.
I can almost see the other side,
Won't you desist from claims a little while?
For recession, I warn, is inevitable,
If you continue to cramp my style.
For mutineers I will not stand, so why not be
My partisans and together help me
Fight the flames of inflation?
For fire fighters we all must be, if we are going to save
Our prosperity which keeps on burning unceasingly,
While we grow enraged, and just disagree.
But Europe, it's got to be as you shall surely see,
For our voices must be heard in the world again,
But this time in harmony with the E.E.C."

POLICE STATE

Oh what a subtle police state, the finest I have seen,
Yet many would doubt that this is so
But fear to venture out,
And in this police state of theirs, to be poor or black is a crime.
And if you don't believe me try driving or walking out after nine,
And if you are so bold as to take this fearless walk
And you are not stopped, harassed, and searched by some wicked cop
It only means that your time has not yet come.
Angered are we, to have our divine right infringed upon like this.
For wherever you may go in a public place,
Like a peeping tom he's there,
But when you truly need him, he can't be found anywhere.
His presence, they will tell you, is to protect society.
And so poor whites and black people are treated as though they are the enemy.
Tired we are of having our liberty trampled upon by such impetuous fools,
And if this is not a subtle police state, then why not quickly change the rule?
Respect the police asked of us, but that I'm sure they'll never get,
For their evil ways they first must change,
And stop being a regular pest.
This police democratic state cares only for the rich ruling class and bourgeois fools
And hates the poor working man and treats him rather cruel.
In China, they will tell us, these things cannot be said,
And remind us of the freedom here,
But destroy us, just as well ...

LAMENTATION

Oh Africa, my heart bleeds for you,
With your bastard sons and daughters,
Products of a nightmarish rape,
For against your ancient wishes
The invaders came and subdued you
And stole your virginity
And made you a harlot against your will.

Oh Africa, I feel the pains of this ominous invasion,
Like a spear wound in my heart,
Unhealing until you are healed. How long must I bleed,
How long must I grieve,
For in your emulation of colonialism,
You are ruining the holy seed.

Oh Africa, stop your prostitution,
Close your legs and rise from this state of dissipation,
Go, baptise yourself in the Nile and the Zambezi
That your callous floundering may cease,
Becoming a warrior of men,
United in the spirit of unity, love and victory.

Oh Africa, the epitome of the West,
How unrecognisable you are
In your strange apparels and habits.
Are you the true ancient mother of mystical glory and wisdom
Whose sons' bodies once contained the hearts of lions,
And whose wills were as strong as the diamond,
Stolen from our land,
Whom danger respected and to whom death was no enemy,
Are you this great, ancient mother of mine?

Oh Africa, stop producing docile imbeciles
And return to ancient cultural mystery
Which you think is obsolete,

And regain the tie with our Creator.
Seek out the seers, wizards, and witch doctors,
Let them invoke angels and demons to put dread in the hearts
Of the enemies that they flee from your sick body
That it may heal.

Oh Africa, beat out the rhythm of love and concern,
Across the seas, on the tom-toms, calling your children home
From these strange and distant lands,
And resuscitate your soul with their presence,
Oh Mother, call, call, and the wise among us shall come.

Oh Africa, how thin you look,
Like a cow that has not eaten for years,
With your blood siphoned away by the vampires
Of capitalism, leaving you wounded and crippled
With thoughts of industrialisation and continued dependence
Upon your enemies.

Oh Africa, listen to the young of the day,
And don't foolishly negotiate their efforts away,
For if blood is the price to rid ourselves of these parasites,
Then let it flow on the sacrificial altar of liberty and truth,
For freedom is achieved in no other way.

Oh Africa, we stand alone in our troubles,
Hated by all, loved by none;
We have no friends, so beware of the gift-bearers,
For in their hearts treachery lies.
Have your wounds been cleansed and bandaged by them,
Have your children been fed to satisfaction by them,
So when will this stinking tumour of foreign influence cease to be?

Oh Africa, how dissected you are,
In your democratic and communistic divisions of lunacy!
Is there no idealism that can bind you as one nation?
Then how about Africanism, united in progression,
Or is this beyond your colonial comprehension,
Or are you ashamed of the wisdom of your mystical heritage?

Oh Africa, how decayed you look in your modernisation,
You abandoned the beautiful gardens of the forest,
Where the birds sing and the animals roam,
Where you resided as men, unafraid,
Sharing your catch in brotherly love,
For the concrete jungle of the technological world,
Robbed of your manhood and senses, to become buffoons.

Oh Africa, have I pained you, my love,
Have you found my words harsh on your tender ears?
Tis only for love of you that I speak these truths of pain and grief,
Of blood and war,
Of death and life.
But death is the beginning of life anew,
So why be afraid, my beloved,
For your King has come, and is of African origin.

Oh Africa, the stench of your corruption is smelt from afar,
Shepherds who should have led my flocks to the green pasture
And crystal clear streams to quench their thirst,
Have deserted for material obscurity,
Causing my flock to stray.

Oh Leaders of Africa, I have arrived, and curse you,
May your bodies start to decay before you are dead,
May the crows pick out your eyes when you are drunk and disorderly,
And may your balls be swollen to stop your fornication,
And the righteous subdue you to shame,
May your wives seek other lovers, who encourage them to poison your food,
May the nice house you live in be swallowed up by an earthquake,
And may your Sons murder you in your sleep,
May your souls be driven to the furthest parts of hell,
And may your Daughters show their lovers your secret places,
So that they lay traps to disembowel you,
May the wife you love best end up with your enemy,
And may the ties you wear around your neck,
Strangle you when the jackass brays,

May the car you drive crash and break every bone in your body,
And may the plane explode next time you fly to Europe,
Killing you and your entourage;
And if you should travel by ship, may it sink and you be eaten by a devil fish,
And if you refuse to open the door to your people,
May the crocodile God pay you a visit,
And you know what to expect when he comes;
And may the wines and spirits you drink tumorise your bodies.

These are the curses of evil brought on the wings of wisdom from deep within me,
From across the waters, where I sit and watch you in my astral eye,
And the spirits of our ancestors rejoice and dance in mystical reunion with Rastafari to see this day.

BE FREE

Use your imagination,
Get rid of the stagnation,
Delve into the inner self,
Find the mysteries
That unlock the door,
That set you free.

With no inhibition,
Why not try this expedition?
Explore the abyss of mind and soul
And as sure as can be,
You'll find the key
That sets you free.

Forget about what the experts say,
They are determined to traverse the opposite way.
Don't let them beguile, and treat you as a child,
For they are the Kings of darkness
Only for a while.

As you travel internally, and see
The invisible chain,
Binding the spirit of nations
In their material delusions,
My heart joyously
In its mystic domain
Will know that you are free.

THE WARRIOR'S END

When the angel of death knocks on my door
He'll find me ready and willing to go.
No hesitation on my part shall there be
When the angel of death comes to do his duty
He'll find me ready and willing to go,
But his coming for me seems oh, so slow.

I'm already prepared and eager to go,
So when Allah sends him I'll open my door,
I'll say to the angel of death, "Come in, my friend,
Just let me make my last Salat,
Then when I'm finished, straight away to
Allah we will go."

When the angel of death knocks on my door
There'll be no objection on my part,
For I've already examined my heart,
I have done what the laws have said,
And I have lived the life of the harmless dead.

So when the angel of death comes on that future day
He'll find me ready, as I've said before, for
I've already prepared myself for when that happy day comes,
For I no longer belong to this dreadful world.

So when the angel of death comes
With Allah's command
I'll be happy to lend him a gentle hand,
My soul from my body I shall happily release,
Like a good jinn, freed from a bottle by a holy priest.

THE BAIT

The desire for material things
Is far stronger than anything I know,
It's stronger than diamond, stronger than steel
And stronger than faith,
Yet it's but an elusion.

And knowing this, the capitalists
Exploit this weakness of man
So he works night and day,
To put new things on display,
And dare us to resist them, knowing
Full well that we can't.

Their showrooms are as hooks,
Baited with different looks,
And as we pass by they capture our eyes,
And we are caught, just like fish in a brook.

WAYS OF LIFE

There are two ways of life,
The right way, and the wrong way.
The right way is the way of God,
And the wrong way is the devil's way,
And he who lives the devil's way
Is denied the Divine Light.
But he who lives the way of God
Has got eternal Life.
And the world today
Is the devil's way
And not the way of God.

So on Judgement Day,
Which is on its way,
Man has got a lot to pay.
And on that day,
What shall you say,
When your life is forfeited
For living the devil's way?

WE ARE ALL WRONG

Why have these divisions,
Why not pursue a united world?
Let us all admit our wrongs
And start again on new ground.
For we are all wrong,
Wrong as we all could be,
So let make a new start, but this time in harmony.
Right away, let's forget who did this, and who did that
And start again with concern for each other.
Because we are all wrong,
Oh admit, admit it,
For the end will surely come.
WE know what we are doing,
WE are civilised, they say.
But tell me, tell me,
Do civilised people really behave this way?
As I look back over the years to when time had first begun,
I can see that man has not changed,
The change is in our weapons
But not within us.
Oh admit you're wrong, admit you're wrong,
For if you don't
The end is sure to come.

A KIDDY'S POEM

I am an egg, standing on my head
Wondering when I shall be eaten,
For gluttonous men have eaten several of my friends
And left me here wondering, will I grow up to be a hen?

Many of my brothers and sisters have been eaten too,
Some were boiled and some were fried,
And some were poached as well.

But who's to say that one day our parents
Will not rebel,
But if by chance I grow up to be a hen
I shall lay and lay and lay.

Please don't eat me.

A KIDDY'S POEM

I'm a little mouse, very carefree at play,
And all I ask of you, my friends,
Is to give me a piece of cheese each day.

This will make me healthy and strong,
I shall not spread my germs around,
For if I go to the dustbin to feast
I know for sure my germs wouldn't cease.

So take this friendly warning from me
And try not to be mean and I shall grow up
To be happy, nice and clean.

So remember what I said and all shall be well.
A piece of cheese from you would be really very swell.

A friend.

PROSE

If only the world would stop and think of God
Before the morning comes,
It would bring them blessings from above,
Instead of a thunderstorm.

A BEGGAR

There are two kinds of beggars:
Those who beg from mankind,
And those who beg from God.
The beggar who begs from mankind,
Begs for wealth.
But the beggar who begs from God,
Begs for wisdom, and in wisdom
HE has wealth.

THIS DARK WORLD

The world lives in darkness
And disaster is inevitable,
For without the divine light
The world shall never see.

THEIR TROUBLED WORLD

The troubles of the world
Are the reflection of men's souls,
And a troubled soul means a troubled world,
And a troubled world is a sick spirit.

SAYINGS

Mankind has heard of God but remains
Reluctant in getting to know him.

We know who the devil's advocates are,
And they are the enemies of God and humanity.

The believers know of God,
But do not know him yet.

And the true servants of God
Acknowledge him and spend their lives
Getting to know him.

God's enemies are everywhere;
In every nation of every race.

The men responsible for creating and
Building edifices are few in numbers
And what they build are enjoyed by kings
And fools alike.

RAIN OF SORROW

As the rain of sorrow
Descends from the sky,
Drenching the earth in solemn glee,
Farmers everywhere are
Contemplating, hoping and cursing,
Every drop of the rain of sorrow.

This is not a blessing,
But a curse, the harvesters cry,
But the true reason for it, they know not why,
While greedy, obese families
Gorge themselves in glee,
Oblivious of the rain of sorrow.

The saturated earth knows for sure,
Disaster knocks at the nation's door,
From its mystic discourse.

Greying and darkened clouds amass
And entomb the city from the sun,
While angry citizens traverse the city streets
Like demented spirits in hell.
The rain of sorrow lulls momentarily,
Awaiting its Creator's command.

If only the sun would shine, they say
Silently in their thoughts,
Though loud enough for the sun to hear
As it shines and smiles in a distant land.

The order came at eight that night,
And down poured the rain of sorrow again,
The city streets now washed clean and bare,
For all the citizens, singly and in pairs,

Have returned to their private tombs
To sleep, in despair,
Cursing the rain of sorrow, as their prayers,
Forgetful of their many other blessings.

THE DEW OF THE FLOWER OF LIGHT

When the dew of the flower of light
Descends through space and time,
And cosmic selections are made,
Pray I always to be amongst those
Whose lips shall taste of her sweetness.
Go, atheist, agnostic, and communist,
And ask the recipients against whose lips she
Slightly brushed,
Penetrating the core of their being,
Making genius of them in an instance.
Oh when the dew of the flower of light
Descends through space and time,
And touches the hearts of men in solitary places,
Pray I always to be amongst those whose spirits
Are saturated with her light.
Go, humanists, naturists, and hypocrites,
And ask her recipients whose souls differentiate
The dual realities,
Finally liberated from systematic bondage, and
Transcending beyond mundane dreams.

THE WHENS OF LIFE

When I met my Creator
I found myself,
I recognised my shortcomings
And rectified myself.

Now when I meet a true Christian
I meet myself,

And when I pray with a loyal Muslim
I pray with myself,

And when I sit with a detached
And honourable Buddhist on the path of truth
I sit with myself.

And when I leave this world
I shall leave by myself.

But when I am confronted by a democrat
I meet my former confusion and his evil intention
Towards me, and humanity,

And when I reason with a communist
I speak to a man that is totally lost in darkness
And is cursed by our Creator and his angels,

And whenever I encounter a true advocate of the Devil,
With his or her deceptive charm,
I know I have a battle on my hands
And they are sure to be defeated.

HOLY MEN

Oh what a pleasure to meet a holy man
In times as vile as these!
He stands out like a gem on earth,
Among these evil creeds,
He wears a heart that's full of love, and
Eyes of diamond brightness.
He shuns the things the world enjoys
And seeks the divine light.
But in this light he sees the world the way
It should not be.
For men have strayed ten thousand years
In their diversity.
And if there were no holy men
To warn us when we stray,
ALLAH knows what would become of us
As we live from day to day.
So I for one have taken heed of what these
Wise men say,
Though others may scoff and doubt and laugh
And drink their lives away.

THE BLESSED

Some men die for their minds to be free,
But those whose minds are free,
And are not dead,
They are Blessed,
So say I ...

SEASONS

Summer is coming to a close,
And soon the deciduous trees
Shall change their coats of green,
To brown and gold.

And oh, what autumn joy they
Shall bring us all this year,
Lifting our spirits and helping
Our souls to soar to God,
And sending a tingling through
Our hearts once more,

Then shedding their beautiful coats
Of brown and gold,
And standing menacingly, naked
Before our very eyes, throughout
Their wintry sleep,

And, three months later, confronting us
In their new coats of lighter green.
As spring comes on nature's wheel
Of life, so the resurrection shall be

As the spring of judgement day comes
When every soul will stand alone
Before God to answer for their deeds,
Of gold, silver, brass and bronze.

DANCING TREES

I've seen the trees dancing today
As the wind engulfed them on its way,
Each tree was doing a dance of its own
And trying not desperately but gracefully
To outdance each other.
And oh, how these trees did dance with such a rhythm
That I had never seen, with their branches swaying
And their leaves performing a thousand
Variations of the dance,
And as the wind subsided
These trees took their former stance
Breathlessly
Awaiting to start again
Their
Sacred
Dance.

CHRISTMAS

Christmas is here,
I can feel it in the air,
The fragrant breeze,
The Christmas trees,
The laughter that I hear.

I can even hear sleigh bells
Ringing from afar
And the choristers singing,
With their eyes fully radiant as the stars.

I can see the busy people
Shopping in their glee,
Everyone seems happy,
As far as I can see.

And I even see Santa Claus
Checking on his list
To make sure that this Christmas
Each child receives a gift.
Christmas is here,
Can you feel it in the air,
The preparation made by parents
For children everywhere.

THE LORD KNOWS

The lord knows
That I know, He does exist,
And I know that the lord knows this.
This, then, is the acknowledgement of my quest
On the path of truth,
That leads to obedience, peace, and rest.
I know that the lord exists,
And I know he's aware that I know this.

ECSTASY

Those ecstatic moments we shared
In the stillness of the night,
While the whole world lay sleeping,
Then in you I found the light.

Companion, teacher and lover,
These things you have been to me,
In the abyss of your love,
I found my destiny.
You taught me everything I know,
Now my life belongs to thee.

I remember when you called, I answered,
Without hesitation I came,
I found you, and in you myself
That short time span ago,
And now with patience I wait
Until that great day comes,
When all the world shall know
That I have found you and I have become your son.

VOICE

The voice of truth
Cries out for revenge.
With retribution in hand,
Now falsehood must end.
While in carefree sinful deeds
The world's nations do proceed
To enjoy the pleasures of the dead,
The command is given,
But unknown to some men:
Destroy as you go,
This era is closed,
And lay a Godly foundation,
Chastise the world with famine, earthquake,
Hurricane, plague, wars and inflation.
But if by chance the world repent,
Show mercy, for that too is at your command.

THE BOOKS

I have two friends
That are so dear to me,
They help me when I worship God,
And to set my mind free.
Free from trouble,
Free from fear,
Free from economy,
Free from politics
And free from despair.
They are friends among friends,
Trustworthy and true
And they stay silently until they are used,
And in their arms they caress wisdom,
Of treasures untold.
I have two friends, that know all things,
Things that are hidden,
Things that are told,
Things that are here and things that are gone,
And of things to come, that are bad and good.
I have two friends
They are a pleasure to consult,
They have all the answers,
The world is in search of,
Answers for love,
Answers for pain,
Answers for hate,
And the answers for peace.
I have two friends,
Whose persons I share with the world,
A blind world,
A foolish world,
And a sad world.
I have two friends,
They are always available,

At any time of day, if you care to look their way,
In the morning, in the evening, and at night time too,
What great friends to have,
If only the world but knew.

REPUDIATE

We've given up our culture
We've given up our faith
We've given up our God
We've given up everything,
And now that we are lost
Isn't time we sit and think?
Look at the stars
Look at the trees
Look at ourselves,
Don't they mean anything?
Our God spoke to me with
Reverence from above.
Hold on, he said, the world is blind,
Sight is given to the divine.
You are mad, they say,
Discreet looks convey your way.
Let them laugh: all the tomorrows
Shall be your day.

SOLITUDE

In my solitude you found me
And you took me by my hand,
And led me down the path of wisdom
And made me a happy man.

And for all these things I thank you
From the bottom of my heart,
You took me from my darkness
And brightened up my path.

Now I'm in harmony with the universe,
Now that you've taken me to your breast
And cast away my fears,
My doubts and my sorrows,
And replenished me with light.

ALLAH'S TRUE LOVE

I love Allah, and he loves me,
And that love, I know, will last throughout eternity.
And whatever I do and whatever I say,
I hope it shall always be in relation
To the Godly way.

For if I do depart, I know it will break his heart,
For a love as ours so divine and true,
Breaking his heart will be breaking mine too.

I love Allah and he loves me, and
I pray that's the way it shall always be.
He has sent us a warning of a new world dawning
To save us from our sin.

So don't let the mirage of success
Blind you from his love,
For I know that he loves you too
As he guides us from above.

I love Allah, but he loves us all
And I pray that I shall never fall.

SPIRIT

If you are the one
I believe you are,
Then you must be my guide and star
Who has come to take me
On a journey, through the universe up high
To see its splendour and mysteries
And to feast my eyes.
Then go right ahead, and take my hand
And lead me to enchanting lands,
Places of joy and mystical ecstasy
Through space and time
I want to be.
If you are the one I think you are
Then you are from above, and very far,
And have come to earth to shower me
With your divine love, mercy and peace.
Then take my hand and lead me there,
For where you are, I long to be,
In your domain, my lord and friend,
To dwell in spiritual reality, with thee,
O Majesty.

THE FORGETFUL

My nights are like daytime,
And daytime is like my nights.
In darkness, I am the light,
In fact, I am the perpetual light.

When men slumber, I watch over them,
When they cry out, in moments of distress,
I take heed of their cry and show mercy,
And although my light is seen,
It is soon forgotten.

Then distress calls at the door once more,
And then I am remembered.
But who's to say that one day
That call may not be answered?
Yet there are some whose path
I guide to infinity.

BE SILENT

Man seeketh everywhere to find the Lord,
Some in faith, others in trust,
But those who seeketh me with truth in their hearts,
Haven't got far to look.

Man has gone to mountain tops seeking me,
Others to far more remote places.
I accompanied them all,
And watched them fail in their mission
And become disbelievers.
But I am not a needle in a haystack,
For I am so much easier to find,
For one can be deprived of physical sight and find
Me just as well.

Now to those who have tried to find me and failed,
And those who shall try to find me,
And those who have already given up all hope of
Finding me,
I say this,
Be silent, and let the Lord thy God speak to you.

YE FOOLS

Ye fools of servants far and near,
I see thee lucidly,
You have repudiated thy clothes and
Not thy sin,
But I still know thee.
You may convey false impressions
And scheme your way into high places,
But to enter the highest place of them all
You need monothought.

A FRIENDLY VOICE

A friendly voice, a friendly voice,
Is what I long to hear,
What voice of prayer of man's deceit
I hear.
An unfriendly voice of prayer
Expects me to lend an ear.

A friendly voice, a friendly voice,
Of earnest prayer to me
Is like music to my ear
Upon the heavenly sea.

I give, I grant,
I love whose prayer comes up to me
With a friendly voice of love.

A friendly voice, a friendly voice,
A divine thought, a divine wish
A divine being
So few is he
And him I bless.

A friendly voice, a friendly voice,
A true Son
A true joy,
Wisdom's treasures he will enjoy.

To the Jurisprudence

The philosophy of law is called Jurisprudence and its aim is to consider the nature, origin and classification of law. And one of the most important ideas of the legal theorists is the idea of natural law. The theory of natural law is based on the belief that there is a set of perfect rules for human conduct and the laws devised by men must be judged by these rules. If by natural law they mean the laws of nature which should govern man's behaviour, which is an Ordinance by Almighty God, why then don't they say so, rather than leaving room for argument by men of a lesser calibre? For what this means is that the laws of conduct given to man in the Holy Scriptures and all man-made laws should be judged by these rules. But contrary to this Divine Ordinance is John Austin's perfidious idea in opposition which claims that law is a command set by a superior being to an inferior being. The superior being is the state and the inferior being the individual, and this makes it possible that when a law is passed by Parliament it is judged by the rule of the legislators with relation to party concept, interest and injustice.

This insidious terminology was given birth by the first professor of jurisprudence at University College, London, John Austin (1790 - 1859). Had this person truthfully described the superior being as God Almighty and the inferior being the state, it would have required men of a pious and higher calibre to sit in judgement over us as individuals and the law and their rulings would have been in relation to natural law, which is God Almighty's law, and not the state, as is predominant in England and other countries of the world which are supposedly Christian and followers of Christ.

This led to another interpretation by another shallow-minded philosopher of Law, John Salmon, who defined law as a body of principles, recognised and applied by the State in the administration of justice again in accordance with the State (whose principles have no relationship with God's laws and could never be justified if one is truly contemplating justice. The same person responsible for the above interpretation defined what a State is as follows: the society of men established for the maintenance of peace and justice within a determined territory by way of force - which we know only too well in the modern world. But the word State defined by me would be a society of honourable and God-fearing men established to administer justice without prejudice, so cultivating peace within a determined territory by impartial judgement and education, eliminating the use of force; for wherever and whenever force is used one can be assured that some human right is being violated by the State, and the aggrieved group or person or nation have bravely stood up against that violation.

I'm obliged to reiterate Sir John Salmon's definition of law, which is the body of principles recognised and applied by the State in the administration of justice. The State is a society of men, established for the maintenance of peace and justice within a determined territory by way of force. But whose body of principles are they, that of God, the devil or man? And we can see clearly that the two political thinkers have omitted the natural laws, which are the Ordinance of God Almighty, from the laws of the State. We are left with the devil and man, and man would be the first to admit that he is not perfect, and therefore there are always going to be flaws in his reasoning which cause great distress to the members of the territories which they govern because of their nepotism and partiality in relation to group interest at the expense of others of his own race, because of the class system, which if they were God-fearing they would not do and which leaves them entirely open to the devil's influence in their analysis of events and in their legislation. So instead of the law and State being of God Almighty it is truly without doubt the State of the devil which all ungodly men serve with such reverence and loyalty to the detriment of those who are governed by them as we can see in the world today wherever we care to direct our thoughts, whether east, west, north or south - wherever the idea of the State being superior and the individual being inferior is accepted and is well established by the devil's advocates, be it democratic or communistic, the result is the same. For where God is not present, there can be no justice.

Such deep-rooted, soul-destroying and dangerous traditions of law and state must be re-examined and rectified by the present generation of today if they are not to follow in the footsteps of their predecessors, who have caused considerable distress, pain and suffering to humanity and have built a very chaotic world by their digression from the true law. And if they don't change and continue on the same lines as their predecessors, then they would have proven themselves no better than their forefathers and would be judged by God Almighty for this grave folly of theirs.

The judges should be men of the highest moral principle, for the men that know what's right must indeed live a better life, and men that do not know must indeed live a wretched life. But there are two kinds of judges, the impartial and the partial: the impartial judge sleeps soundly at night, for he is at peace with himself and his soul is at rest, but the partial judge does battle with his conscience and his soul is in turmoil. So too with the Legislators of the world.

The Democratic concept is like a cancer of the mind and it eats away our morality

The democratic concept of life is analogous to a cancer of the mind. It eats away the morality of man and transforms the individual and nation's character so that it become unrecognisably human and more like the animal Darwin claims he is.

And as a cancer eats away at the patient body until the death of he or she occurs, so too humanity would die if morality and God are not returned to expeditiously, for without these two ingredients how will it be possible to save humanity?

The importance of morality cannot be sufficiently emphasised here, for morality is the guideline, the rudder, the compass that keeps the nation cohering together on its course. And its absence from the democratic concept is surely responsible for the democratic people's psychological ills and dispositions: for example, to live in constant fear, dualism, mistrust and xenophobia towards other races, especially the darker skinned people of the world, particularly the African.

And to be without morality is to be without God, and to be without God is to be without morality, and as the nation divorces itself from

God so too morality disappears. This is true of the Western and Eastern societies of the world today and cannot be denied by anyone because it is scientifically true and proven so; for all the world's social, political, economic, judicial, educational, domestic and cultural ills and cruel inconsiderate, treacherous and evil behaviour stares us in the face. And I am quite certain that if the organs of a man's body were as diseased and sick as any of these institutions, he would be advised to have immediate surgery by the most efficient surgeon, one in whom he can trust. And the most efficient surgeon, I stress emphatically, to perform this operation on the democratic and communistic man must be God Almighty; and the sooner humanity, the patient, presents himself by returning to him, the quicker the ills of the societies of the world will be gotten rid of.

This would make it possible for both East and West to experience this spiritually and scientifically by returning to God. So that together we can all observe the wonderful healing of the nations, which no scientific body would be able to deny.

To begin the first step along this road of the nations of the world healing, let every king, judge, politician and all professional men, civil servants, parents and children, men and women live by The Ten Commandments, as a start, for in these Commandments lies the law of morality which are the principles for the perfections of oneself, and on to the next stage to the true Islam, where we find the followers of Moses, Christ, Mohammed and Buddha. Peace be upon them all, would live together in peace and brotherly love under Islam as one brotherhood as intended by Our Creator, the Merciful, the Magnificent.

It is pointless for any man or woman to utter that famous line, that man cannot change.

Man is man, so I know he cannot change, but he sure can change from being an animal and become human, which is the lift humanity needs in its travails between death and extinction. And our survival is only made possible by returning to Our God, through repentance. Let the leaders of the governments of the world take heed, for they shall have to answer to God for all the unnecessary suffering caused to humanity by their atheism, which causes them to stumble in the darkness. In their struggles to establish their deceptive class interest they even legislated against the laws of God in parliament, which to me is a combination of blindness and stupidity and a further step away from God Almighty, which eventually must bring doom to the nation they govern and the state.

Excessive Hoarding of Wealth and its Repercussion

The capitalists have an obligation to the poor and needy of the world, but it seems that they think that the poor and needy were put on this planet earth for the sole purpose of exploitation by them. This misconception must be revised for humanity's sake. The excessive hoarding of wealth is mostly responsible for the poverty we see and experience in the world around us.

Today in Africa, South America and India we have million of people living under the most atrocious conditions and millions of others starving to death, whilst the rich families of the world hoard their wealth with no sense of responsibility to their fellow men and with the governments spending vast sums of money on military hardware and space programme and hoarding the surplus in their treasuries to their own people's detriment, completely ignoring the fact that if money is not allowed to circulate to every member of the society, that there is going to be trouble for such a society. Those who can evaluate the disparity and have missed out on education are obviously going to turn to crime. And the other members of society who have not the constitution and ability remain in dire poverty, as you can see in Europe, North and South America, India and Africa.

The government of the rich countries of the world along with the rich families should be ashamed of themselves. What type of people are they whom we employ to represent us in government? What type of people are they that they could be so inconsiderate to the poor of the planet and pretend to be members of the human race, which they are certainly not, for human beings must be more considerate. For the code given by God to man is to love for your brother what you love for yourself or love your brother as you love yourself as was said by both

Christ and Mohammed, Peace be upon them, and until this code is achieved within themselves the richest men and women and ministers of the governments and their subordinates must exclude themselves from the human race, which more or less they have done already anyway, for they hoard their wealth and cause millions to starve. They seem to lack the ability to comprehend the idea that the necessary circulation of money in a society is as important as the circulation of blood in the body, and when cut off from any point of the body causes discomfort or even death. So too when the government tightens the purse-strings, as they are now doing universally, it causes discomfort, great suffering, pain, delusions and death to members of the lower rungs of society, and can never be justifiable by any excuses they conspire to tell us. For actions speak louder than words and the truth is they couldn't care less in their "I'm alright Jack" concept of the lesser human person.

In the Name of God, Most Gracious, Most Merciful
Putting Right the Wrong

Statements made by some Intellectuals and Scientists

When my contemporaries state emphatically that I am an idealist, because of my concept of life, with a hint of condemnation and rejection in their voices, as most people who have not any idea of their own do, whether they be educated or not, I say to them with love and the kindness of my heart that nothing was ever brought into being without it first being an idea given to man by either God or the Devil and I kindly draw their attention to the democratic ideas which they so lovingly embrace and adhere to because it liberates them from all moral responsibility, and say that this too is idealistic, often brought into being by force and threats if necessary.

I also say this to those who cling to the idea of the Scientists, who say nothing should be accepted until proven scientifically (by them themselves). What, I ask my contemporaries, is a man to do with his empirical experience of our Creator? Dismiss this wonderful and enlightened blessed moment of the once in a lifetime communication to every generation from the time of Adam to an individual whom the Creator summons to listen to Him, in this case me, and now you?

Should I dismiss this and wait upon the scientists to confirm my own experience? They who are blinded by their own atheism, where is the logic in this? When the Creator has already confirmed His existence to me, am I to give the scientists' thinking priority over my own? No, not in this instance, for my own experience is spiritual and they lack the temperament to accomplish any results in this reality, therefore his conclusions have no validity to me in this domain, king though they may be in the physical reality of their concrete domain, where I never trespass.

For the science of the two realities requires different approaches and dispositions by those who wish to enter them.

For example, the person who wishes to pursue the truth from the physical reality starts from the position of doubt, later cultivating arrogance and self-importance, which is clear in the ridiculous statements made to substantiate the half-truth to turn the society to their way of thinking.

For example, some years ago in the early nineties an allegation was made by the scientific fraternity challenging the age or time it took for completing the creation of the earth, which was calculated to be six thousand years old by both Christians and Muslims alike for the past two thousand years.

We created heaven and earth and all between them in six days nor did any sense of weariness touch us. Sura L Ayat 38; Genesis Chapter 1, vv. 1 - 31.

Now apparently the scientists discovered a carbon process technique called carbon dating by which they can determine the age of material things and after laborious testing of a quantity of earth, concluded that the earth was millions of years older than what the Bible and Koran imply and which the Leaders of the world's two great religions remain reticent about. However, the question I wish to raise to vindicate the two prophets and strengthen the followers' faith in the two holy books is this: if you were to cut down a tree that was a thousand years old, had it lumbered and then built a new house that took six months to complete, and someone were to ask you how old is your house, you are not going to say to the person that your home is a thousand years old because it was built from a tree that old, surely not. You would tell the person it was six months old, which stands to reason.

Another example is, if I were to have taken a quantity of flour that was seven years old or for that matter a thousand years old, which was well preserved, and bake a bread on a Friday and was asked how old it was on the Monday, my reply, as well as yours, would be four days old, because the age of the flour does not contravene the age of the bread.

So it is the same with the earth. The material that our merciful Creator used to create the earth could be millions and millions of years old, but the earth itself surely was created in six days, as is mentioned in the holy books, millions of years ago. Yet my contemporaries had the audacity to challenge the authenticity of these two great books and deliberately tried to weaken the faith of the believers of the world and got away with it unchallenged until now. The lord never gave a specific time when he created the earth. All he said was it was created in six days.

And finally as an example, if the scientists wanted to enhance their relationship with the religious fraternity, they would have approached the subject in a more appropriate way, and avoided confrontation by simply saying that God took six thousand earthly years, which is the equivalent of six heavenly days, to complete the creation of the earth millions of years ago. This would have precipitated a different argument altogether, such as the age of man and why he has not developed a more charitable disposition after so many years, but instead the scientists attempted to denigrate the holy books with their carbon dating.

People who are aware of the spiritual reality would have a completely different disposition in their pursuit of the truth, and from a position of belief would cultivate humility and respect for the Creator as they seek to know the truth, with truth also in their hearts, which my contemporaries do not understand or care to.

By Dr Spirit, humble servant of the Lord most high.

The Believer's Argument against the Anthropologist

The anthropologist concluded that man is an animal from his study of man. But I say, man is not an animal, he is a human or spiritual being.

My argument to substantiate this claim lies in the fact that justice cannot be a trait of an animal, and if we are considered to be animals, the judiciary system cannot justify its existence. For why should people who are told that they are animals behave any differently, and why should they be punished, when this same behaviour in the animal world is considered as normal. For when an animal kills or steals from another in the animal world, it is not considered to be a crime by us, or for that matter by the animal world. Why then, when a man perpetrates these same acts in his environment, is he considered a criminal or a beastly person, whom the society, it is said, should be protected from? This then must be considered as unreasonable, for man, if he is an animal, must be judged by the laws of the animal world. In which case he would not be penalised for any of his actions, however vicious his action.

So this idea that man is an animal, if not a deliberate conspiracy to deceive and misdirect, is a tremendous mistake and should be rectified by those people who happen to be our educators and leaders.

For the first judiciary system was set up to adjudicate among a people as a means of keeping the peace and a Divine Ordinance was given to man by God, which is entirely different from that of the animal kingdom where the law of survival of the fittest prevails.

So if a man is to behave as a human being, he must not be told that he is an animal and then penalised by the judiciary that was meant to judge human affairs when he acts as an animal, for this, is contradictory thinking on the thinker's part and a gross injustice.

Now let's see how this misconception that man is an animal came about. My first inclination is that it began with doubt about man's origin, travelling on the stream of disbelief down through the ages to the seventeenth century and on to the era of the anthropologist Darwin, comparing man's behaviour with that of the animals, and recognising similar parental behavioural patterns, for example, parental providence, protectiveness and the means by which offspring comes about, which begins his classification, which I need not go into here. But this eventually led him to trace man's origin to the baboon species of the animal kingdom, which he had become because of his denial of God, and he was completely ignorant of the fact that man has slipped off his psychic plane unto the psychic plane of the animal world, which dictates their behaviour, and so he concluded that man is an animal because of this descent to their level, when turning away from the truth of creation caused him to lose his way.

So whoever then is behind this grievous conspiracy to deceive man that he is an animal and tried to substantiate this misleading idea with the theory of evolution, must be considered criminal and a true danger to humanity, which we can see staring us in the face wherever we look. Commencing from the top, we have religious conflicts, to add to that we have democratic and communist conflict, then the political parties' conflict of each country and the government conflicts of the world.

The conflict between rich and poor, the conflict between workers and management, the conflict between the electorate and the government, the conflict between the police and citizens of the state. All these conflicts are a tremendous task, far too complex for people who proclaim to be animals to resolve.

There is also the conflict between woman and man, children and parents, the young and the old, the victims of rape, muggers, bank robbers and child molesters, which can only be solved when man desists from seeing himself as an animal, but as a human being. For it is no use human-kind crying out in a society which holds the concepts of animalism in place of humanism, not to mention Godism, for in the animal world all problems are solved by the stronger devouring the weaker. Which is exactly what's happening with societies of the world today; for example the rulers of the world, east and west are quite prepared to crush the dissenters, strikers and political demonstrators, ignoring the human causes of their grievances, with the forces of the armies or police, as was recently seen in China and some years ago in Britain by the police against the miners, which is a clear indication of the stronger against the weaker animals. This is the characteristic of the animal world where all carnivorous animals protect their own young, while devouring the young of other species, which are quite harmless and are vegetarian, but that does not stop them from being eaten, for that's the law of the jungle. And so when human beings choose to conduct their affairs along these lines of security of their own, and at the expense of others, how could there ever be peace and justice in the world of man and within man himself? This insidious conditioning concept of man being an animal, so profoundly assimilated among the educated members of the societies of the world, and are being constantly reminded by politicians that we are political animals, and not human beings, indicate the depth that man has descended to and the condition humanity is in.

And the human cry from these inhumane societies for a better world should indicate to our educators in their marvellous academic institutions of learning that they have educated man down the wrong road on the path of life. In (what I would call) their liberalism or deliberation, conspiracy or ignorance, or innocence, were they the victims of the deceptor Satan who whispers into the heart of man and then withdraws after his misguidance (Biblical), or are they fully-fledged subordinates of the deceptor the Devil, who actually blames man for his expulsion from heaven and who actually was the cause of man failing from grace in the first place and the sworn enemy of man?

The leaders' and educators' attitudes have created an ambivalence in the minds of the thinking citizen. The educators, however, were only faced with the dilemma of choosing between good and evil, God or the devil, and their choice is clear now.

Man can either have an anything goes survival society for the fittest which is animalistic, or a caring, considerate and law-abiding, loving, merciful, generous, just and gracious society. By transcending back to his psychic plane under the Divine Ordinance, which brings my arguments to a close and makes a very strong case for us humans to those who have gone astray and who stand as the strongest animals among my fellow man. I beg of you to change your attitude and this satanic behaviour, for there is sufficient wealth of the lands and sustenance given to us by God for all of mankind.

All it really requires is for the animalistic capitalist to be more considerate in the distribution of the wealth of this planet.

And although in the animalistic mind it would seem an unreasonable request, in the mind of the human it isn't, for sharing the world's blessings with one's weaker brother or sister or less developed nations makes us more of a human being, and if the cynics, pessimists and other people in high places believe this to be impossible, then humanity is doomed.

How could you have predators and preys in a human society similar to that of the animal kingdom, for man must differentiate the difference between what's human and what's not.

This statement then is the finality of my argument as a human being and the demand for change. There can be no more excuses.

* * *

This is a call on all Western democratic countries to assist the President of South Africa Nelson Mandela in his hour of need, with all their hearts, so that he can fulfil his promise to his people, who have suffered tremendously under an Apartheid regime and now have to suffer under a democratic one, with their brothers at the head.

Surely you would think that the European nations would help make it possible for him to carry out his housing policy at least, to improve his people's living conditions.

The South African whites themselves should have embraced this opportunity and made a sacrifice by both giving cash and labour to assist the President in providing decent homes for his people.

Taking into consideration the extents he resorted to in legitimising their position in South Africa, one would have thought they would have jumped at the opportunity of helping him to appease his people. But as we can see, the western democracies, along with their unreasonable South African brothers, would prefer him to fail. What a race, what a people, what fools, how unloving, how uncaring, how selfish, how inhuman and how Democratic!

I say that if the West is truly Mandela's friend and wants or wishes him to succeed, then give him the help, by providing the housing materials needed to build these homes for his people, and let him fulfil his dreams.

The western world, in return for all that it has taken from Africa, and is still taking, should give something back now, while it has the chance to do so.

I call on France, Germany, Holland, Belgium, Italy, Spain, Britain and America. For these are the countries that benefited for centuries and whom I await to see making this auspicious gesture so they can return to the human race.

Let the western democrats and the Islamic world give priority to this special and urgently political cause of these needy people.

We have the labour force, give us the material and so let the new world order begin, in peace and love, and consideration.

Dr Spirit ...

A spiritual chart showing the fall of humanity and from where humanity has to transcend, for reconciliation with God, on the path of truth, which is the way of the prophets. But the leaders of the secular world follow the way of the philosophers that has led humanity to its present fall and predicament.

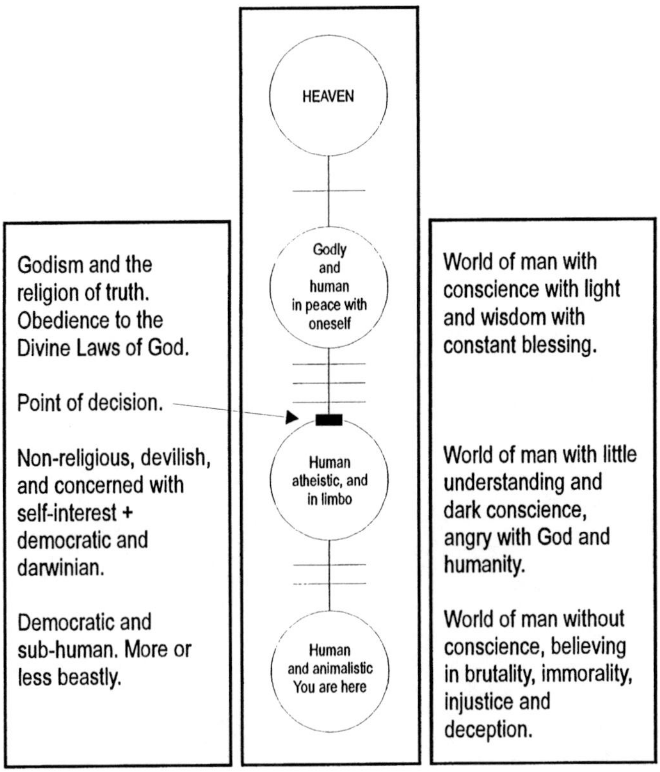

By Dr Spirit ...

The Automatic Hand